PROJECTS FOR NETSCAPE® COMMUNICATOR 4.0

Gillian R. Hall

ADDISON-WESLEY

An imprint of Addison Wesley Longman, Inc.

Reading, Massachusetts • Menlo Park, California • New York • Harlow, England
Don Mills, Ontario • Sydney • Mexico City • Madrid • Amsterdam

Senior Editor: Carol Crowell
Production Supervisor: Juliet Silveri
Copyeditor: Joseph Pomerance
Proofreader: Roseann Viano
Technical Editor: Dawn Remmel
Cover Design Supervisor: Gina Hagen
Marketing Manager: Michelle Hudson
Manufacturing Manager: Hugh Crawford

This book was reproduced by Addison-Wesley from electronic files supplied by the author.

ISBN 0-201-30419-8

Ordering from the SELECT System
For more information on ordering and pricing policies for the SELECT Lab Series and supplements, please contact your Addison Wesley Longman sales representative or call 1-800-552-2499.

Addison-Wesley Publishing Company
One Jacob Way
Reading, MA 01867
http://hepg.awl.com/select
is@awl.com

3 4 5 6 7 8 9 10-DOW-009998

Preface to the Instructor

Welcome to the *SELECT Lab Series.* This applications series is designed to make learning easy and enjoyable, a natural outcome of thoughtful, meaningful activity. The goal for the series is to create a learning environment in which students can explore the essentials of software applications, use critical thinking, and gain confidence and proficiency.

Greater access to ideas and information is changing the way people work. With today's business and communication application software, you have greater integration capabilities and easier access to Internet resources than ever before. The *SELECT Lab Series* helps you take advantage of these valuable resources, with assignments devoted to the Internet and with additional connectivity resources that can be accessed through our Web site, **http://hepg.awl.com/select**.

The *SELECT Lab Series* offers dozens of proven and class-tested materials, from the latest operating systems and browsers, to the most popular applications software for word processing, spreadsheets, databases, presentation graphics, desktop publishing, and integrated packages, to the Internet, e-mail, and HTML authoring, to programming. For your lab course, you can choose what you want to combine; your choice of lab manuals will be sent to the bookstore, combined in a TechSuite, allowing students to purchase all books in one convenient package at a discount.

The most popular *SELECT Lab Series* titles are available in three levels of coverage. The *SELECT Brief* features four projects that quickly lay the foundation of an application in 3 to 5 contact hours. The *standard edition SELECT* expands on material covered in the brief edition with five to eight projects that teach intermediate skills in just 6 to 9 contact hours. *SELECT Plus* provides 10 to 12 projects that cover intermediate to advanced material in 12 to 14 contact hours.

Your Addison Wesley Longman representative will be happy to work with you and your bookstore manager to provide the most current menu of *SELECT Lab Series* offerings, outline the ordering process, and provide pricing, ISBNs, and delivery information. Or call 1-800-447-2226 or visit our Web site at http://www.awl.com

Organization

The "Overview of Windows 95," which appears in some *SELECT Lab Series* modules, familiarizes students with Windows 95 before launching into the application. Students learn the basics of starting Windows 95, using a mouse, using the essential features of Windows 95, getting help, and exiting Windows 95.

Each application is then covered in depth in a number of projects that teach beginning to intermediate skills. An overview introduces the basic concepts of the application and provides hands-on instructions to put students to work using the application immediately. Students learn problem-solving techniques while working through projects that provide practical, real-life scenarios that they can relate to.

Web assignments appear throughout the text at the end of each project, giving students practice using the Internet.

Approach

The *SELECT Lab Series* uses a document-centered approach to learning. Each project begins with a list of measurable objectives, a realistic scenario called the Challenge and a well-defined plan called the Solution. Each project is arranged in carefully divided, highly visual objective-based tasks that foster confidence and self-reliance. Each project closes with a wrap-up of the project called the Conclusion, followed by a summary, questions, exercises, and assignments geared to reinforcing the information taught through the project.

Other Features

In addition to the document-centered, visual approach of each project, this book contains the following features:

- An overview of the application so that students feel comfortable and confident as they function in the working environment.
- Keycaps and toolbar button icons within each step so that the student can quickly perform the required action.
- A comprehensive and well-organized end-of-the-project Summary and Exercises section for reviewing, integrating, and applying new skills.
- An illustration or description of the results of each step so that students know they're on the right track all the time.

Supplements

You get extra support for this text from supplemental materials, including the *Instructor's Manual* and the Instructor's Data Disk.

The *Instructor's Manual* includes a Test Bank for each project in the student text, Expanded Student Objectives, Answers to Study Questions, and Additional Assessment Techniques. The Test Bank contains two separate tests with answers and consists of multiple-choice, true/false, and fill-in questions referenced to pages in the student text. Transparency Masters illustrate key concepts and screen captures from the text.

The Instructor's Data Disk contains student data files, completed data files for Review Exercises and Assignments, and the test files from the *Instructor's Manual* in ASCII format.

For Internet and browser-related lab manuals see the SELECT Web site for supplementary materials.

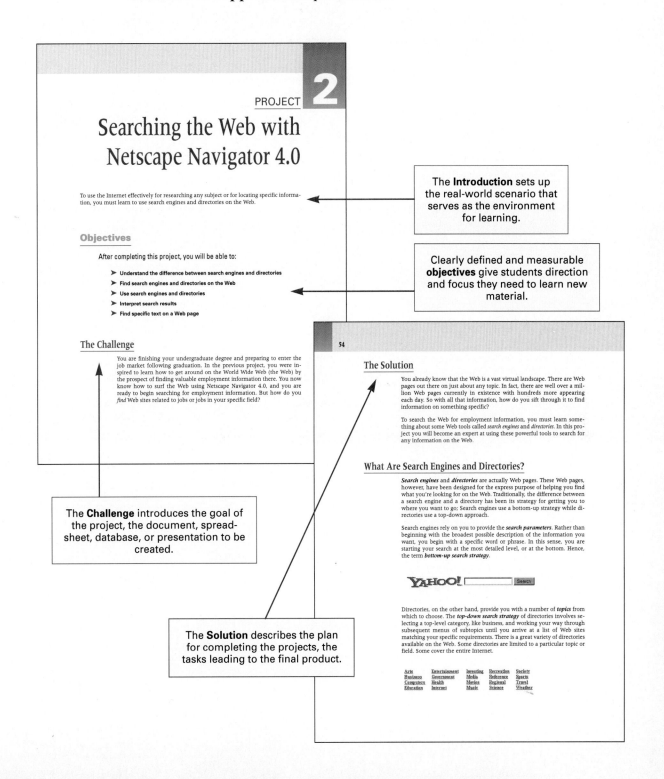

PROJECT **2**

Searching the Web with Netscape Navigator 4.0

To use the Internet effectively for researching any subject or for locating specific information, you must learn to use search engines and directories on the Web.

Objectives

After completing this project, you will be able to:

➤ Understand the difference between search engines and directories
➤ Find search engines and directories on the Web
➤ Use search engines and directories
➤ Interpret search results
➤ Find specific text on a Web page

The Challenge

You are finishing your undergraduate degree and preparing to enter the job market following graduation. In the previous project, you were inspired to learn how to get around on the World Wide Web (the Web) by the prospect of finding valuable employment information there. You now know how to surf the Web using Netscape Navigator 4.0, and you are ready to begin searching for employment information. But how do you *find* Web sites related to jobs or jobs in your specific field?

54

The Solution

You already know that the Web is a vast virtual landscape. There are Web pages out there on just about any topic. In fact, there are well over a million Web pages currently in existence with hundreds more appearing each day. So with all that information, how do you sift through it to find information on something specific?

To search the Web for employment information, you must learn something about some Web tools called *search engines* and *directories*. In this project you will become an expert at using these powerful tools to search for any information on the Web.

What Are Search Engines and Directories?

Search engines and *directories* are actually Web pages. These Web pages, however, have been designed for the express purpose of helping you find what you're looking for on the Web. Traditionally, the difference between a search engine and a directory has been its strategy for getting you to where you want to go; Search engines use a bottom-up strategy while directories use a top-down approach.

Search engines rely on you to provide the *search parameters*. Rather than beginning with the broadest possible description of the information you want, you begin with a specific word or phrase. In this sense, you are starting your search at the most detailed level, or at the bottom. Hence, the term *bottom-up search strategy*.

YAHOO! [_____] [Search]

Directories, on the other hand, provide you with a number of *topics* from which to choose. The *top-down search strategy* of directories involves selecting a top-level category, like business, and working your way through subsequent menus of subtopics until you arrive at a list of Web sites matching your specific requirements. There is a great variety of directories available on the Web. Some directories are limited to a particular topic or field. Some cover the entire Internet.

Arts	Entertainment	Investing	Recreation	Society
Business	Government	Media	Reference	Sports
Computers	Health	Movies	Regional	Travel
Education	Internet	Music	Science	Weather

The **Introduction** sets up the real-world scenario that serves as the environment for learning.

Clearly defined and measurable **objectives** give students direction and focus they need to learn new material.

The **Challenge** introduces the goal of the project, the document, spreadsheet, database, or presentation to be created.

The **Solution** describes the plan for completing the projects, the tasks leading to the final product.

vi

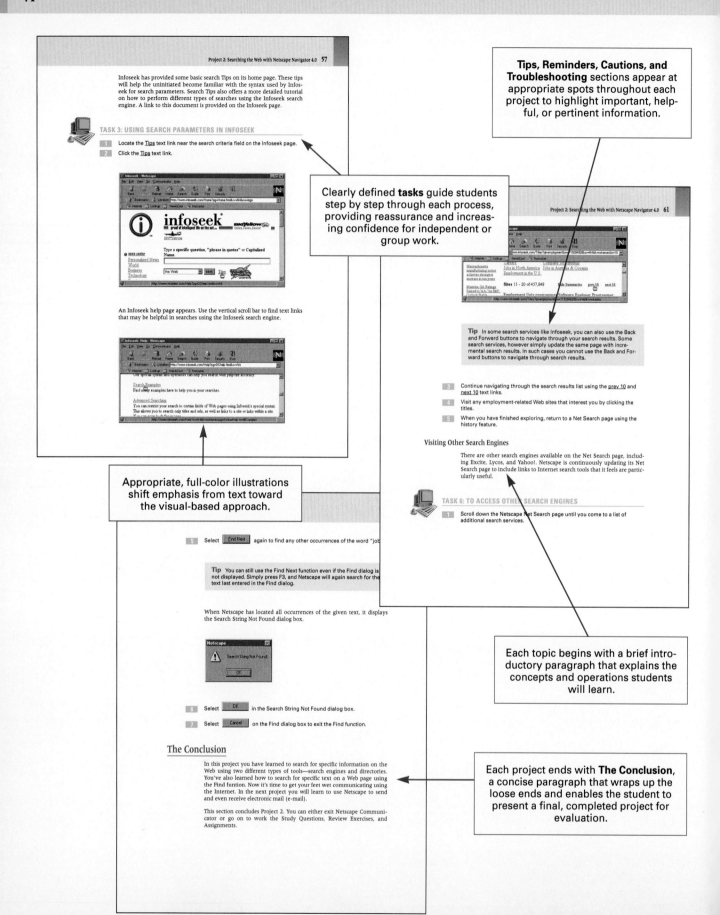

Infoseek has provided some basic search Tips on its home page. These tips will help the uninitiated become familiar with the syntax used by Infoseek for search parameters. Search Tips also offers a more detailed tutorial on how to perform different types of searches using the Infoseek search engine. A link to this document is provided on the Infoseek page.

TASK 3: USING SEARCH PARAMETERS IN INFOSEEK

1. Locate the <u>Tips</u> text link near the search criteria field on the Infoseek page.
2. Click the <u>Tips</u> text link.

An Infoseek help page appears. Use the vertical scroll bar to find text links that may be helpful in searches using the Infoseek search engine.

Tips, Reminders, Cautions, and Troubleshooting sections appear at appropriate spots throughout each project to highlight important, helpful, or pertinent information.

Clearly defined **tasks** guide students step by step through each process, providing reassurance and increasing confidence for independent or group work.

Appropriate, full-color illustrations shift emphasis from text toward the visual-based approach.

Tip In some search services like Infoseek, you can also use the Back and Forward buttons to navigate through your search results. Some search services, however simply update the same page with incremental search results. In such cases you cannot use the Back and Forward buttons to navigate through search results.

3. Continue navigating through the search results list using the <u>prev 10</u> and <u>next 10</u> text links.
4. Visit any employment-related Web sites that interest you by clicking the titles.
5. When you have finished exploring, return to a Net Search page using the history feature.

Visiting Other Search Engines

There are other search engines available on the Net Search page, including Excite, Lycos, and Yahoo!. Netscape is continuously updating its Net Search page to include links to Internet search tools that it feels are particularly useful.

TASK 6: TO ACCESS OTHER SEARCH ENGINES

1. Scroll down the Netscape Net Search page until you come to a list of additional search services.

Each topic begins with a brief introductory paragraph that explains the concepts and operations students will learn.

5. Select [Find Next] again to find any other occurrences of the word "job

Tip You can still use the Find Next function even if the Find dialog is not displayed. Simply press F3, and Netscape will again search for the text last entered in the Find dialog.

When Netscape has located all occurrences of the given text, it displays the Search String Not Found dialog box.

6. Select [OK] in the Search String Not Found dialog box.
7. Select [Cancel] on the Find dialog box to exit the Find function.

The Conclusion

In this project you have learned to search for specific information on the Web using two different types of tools—search engines and directories. You've also learned how to search for specific text on a Web page using the Find funtion. Now it's time to get your feet wet communicating using the Internet. In the next project you will learn to use Netscape to send and even receive electronic mail (e-mail).

This section concludes Project 2. You can either exit Netscape Communicator or go on to work the Study Questions, Review Exercises, and Assignments.

Each project ends with **The Conclusion**, a concise paragraph that wraps up the loose ends and enables the student to present a final, completed project for evaluation.

A bulleted **summary** list further reinforces the objectives and the material presented in the project.

Key terms are boldface and italicized throughout each project and then listed for handy review in the summary section at the end of the project.

Review exercises present hands-on tasks for building on the skills acquired in the project.

Over twenty **study questions** (Multiple Choice, Short Answer, and For Discussion) bring the content of the project into focus again and allow for independent or group review of the material learned.

Assignments invoke critical thinking and encourage integration of project skills.

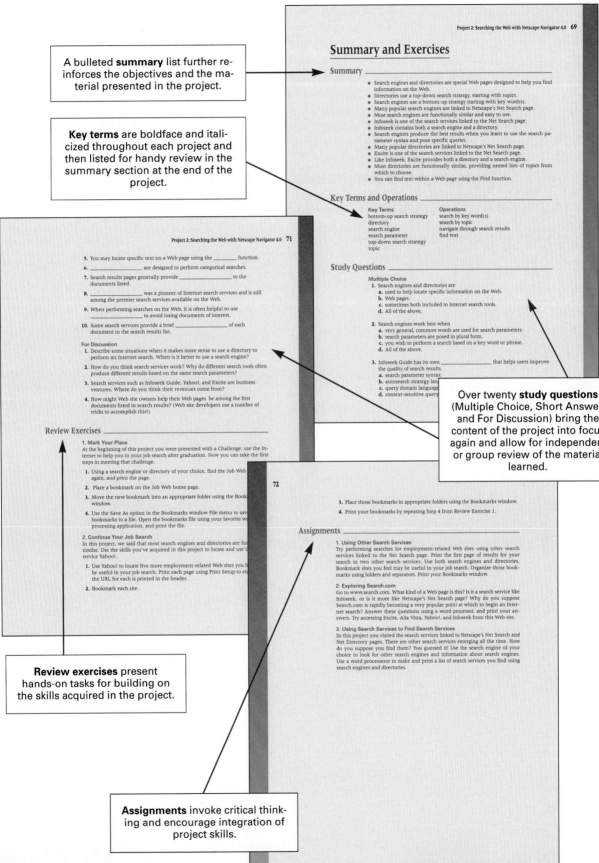

Project 2: Searching the Web with Netscape Navigator 4.0 **69**

Summary and Exercises

Summary

- Search engines and directories are special Web pages designed to help you find information on the Web.
- Directories use a top-down search strategy, starting with topics.
- Search engines use a bottom-up strategy starting with key word(s).
- Many popular search engines are linked to Netscape's Net Search page.
- Most search engines are functionally similar and easy to use.
- Infoseek is one of the search services linked to the Net Search page.
- Infoseek contains both a search engine and a directory.
- Search engines produce the best results when you learn to use the search parameter syntax and pose specific queries.
- Many popular directories are linked to Netscape's Net Search page.
- Excite is one of the search services linked to the Net Search page.
- Like Infoseek, Excite provides both a directory and a search engine.
- Most directories are functionally similar, providing nested lists of topics from which to choose.
- You can find text within a Web page using the Find function.

Key Terms and Operations

Key Terms	Operations
bottom-up search strategy	search by key word(s)
directory	search by topic
search engine	navigate through search results
search parameter	find text
top-down search strategy	
topic	

Study Questions

Multiple Choice

1. Search engines and directories are
   a. used to help locate specific information on the Web.
   b. Web pages.
   c. sometimes both included in Internet search tools.
   d. All of the above.

2. Search engines work best when
   a. very general, common words are used for search parameters.
   b. search parameters are posed in plural form.
   c. you wish to perform a search based on a key word or phrase.
   d. All of the above.

3. Infoseek Guide has its own _____ that helps users improve the quality of search results.
   a. search parameter syntax
   b. autosearch strategy language
   c. query domain language
   d. context-sensitive query

Project 2: Searching the Web with Netscape Navigator 4.0 **71**

5. You may locate specific text on a Web page using the _____ function.

6. _____ are designed to perform categorical searches.

7. Search results pages generally provide _____ to the documents listed.

8. _____ was a pioneer of Internet search services and is still among the premier search services available on the Web.

9. When performing searches on the Web, it is often helpful to use _____ to avoid losing documents of interest.

10. Some search services provide a brief _____ of each document in the search results list.

For Discussion

1. Describe some situations when it makes more sense to use a directory to perform an Internet search. When is it better to use a search engine?

2. How do you think search services work? Why do different search tools often produce different results based on the same search parameters?

3. Search services such as Infoseek Guide, Yahoo!, and Excite are business ventures. Where do you think their revenues come from?

4. How might Web site owners help their Web pages be among the first documents listed in search results? (Web site developers use a number of tricks to accomplish this!)

Review Exercises

1. Mark Your Place
At the beginning of this project you were presented with a Challenge: use the Internet to help you in your job search after graduation. Now you can take the first steps in meeting that challenge.

1. Using a search engine or directory of your choice, find the Job Web [home page] again, and print the page.

2. Place a bookmark on the Job Web home page.

3. Move the new bookmark into an appropriate folder using the Book[marks] window.

4. Use the Save As option in the Bookmarks window File menu to save [your] bookmarks to a file. Open the bookmarks file using your favorite w[ord] processing application, and print the file.

2. Continue Your Job Search
In this project, we said that most search engines and directories are fu[nctionally] similar. Use the skills you've acquired in this project to locate and use t[he] service Yahoo!.

1. Use Yahoo! to locate five more employment-related Web sites you f[eel may] be useful in your job search. Print each page using Print Setup to e[nsure] the URL for each is printed in the header.

2. Bookmark each site.

72

3. Place those bookmarks in appropriate folders using the Bookmarks window.

4. Print your bookmarks by repeating Step 4 from Review Exercise 1.

Assignments

1. Using Other Search Services
Try performing searches for employment-related Web sites using other search services linked to the Net Search page. Print the first page of results for your search in two other search services. Use both search engines and directories. Bookmark sites you feel may be useful in your job search. Organize those bookmarks using folders and separators. Print your Bookmarks window.

2. Exploring Search.com
Go to www.search.com. What kind of a Web page is this? Is it a search service like Infoseek, or is it more like Netscape's Net Search page? Why do you suppose Search.com is rapidly becoming a very popular point at which to begin an Internet search? Answer these questions using a word processor, and print your answers. Try accessing Excite, Alta Vista, Yahoo!, and Infoseek from this Web site.

3. Using Search Services to Find Search Services
In this project you visited the search services linked to Netscape's Net Search and Net Directory pages. There are other search services emerging all the time. How do you suppose you find them? You guessed it! Use the search engine of your choice to look for other search engines and information about search engines. Use a word processesor to make and print a list of search services you find using search engines and directories.

Thanks to . . .

To **Carol Crowell** and **Amy Golash**, thanks for the focus and flexibility needed to get this project off the ground and to keep it airborne.

Special thanks to **Juliet Silveri**, Production Supervisor extraordinaire, whose guidance and support throughout this project are gratefully acknowledged. Thanks also to **Joe Vetere** for all his help in making sure the art in this book looks its best. Thanks to **Joseph Pomerance** for his excellent copy editing and to **Roseann Viano** for her thorough proof-reading. To **Dawn Remmel**, thanks for the tireless technical editing.

Finally, thanks to **David Crockett** for getting me started down this path.

G.R.H.

Acknowledgments

Addison-Wesley Publishing Company would like to thank the following reviewers for their valuable contributions to the *SELECT Lab Series*.

James Agnew Northern Virginia Community College	**Joseph Aieta** Babson College	**Dr. Muzaffar Ali** Bellarmine College	**Tom Ashby** Oklahoma CC
Bob Barber Lane CC	**Robert Caruso** Santa Rosa Junior College	**Robert Chi** California State Long Beach	**Jill Davis** State University of New York at Stony Brook
Fredia Dillard Samford University	**Peter Drexel** Plymouth State College	**David Egle** University of Texas, Pan American	**Linda Ericksen** Lane Community College
Jonathan Frank Suffolk University	**Patrick Gilbert** University of Hawaii	**Maureen Greenbaum** Union County College	**Sally Ann Hanson** Mercer County CC
Sunil Hazari East Carolina University	**Gloria Henderson** Victor Valley College	**Bruce Herniter** University of Hartford	**Rick Homkes** Purdue University
Lisa Jackson Henderson CC	**Martha Johnson (technical reviewer)** Delta State University	**Cynthia Kachik** Santa Fe CC	**Bennett Kramer** Massasoit CC
Charles Lake Faulkner State Junior College	**Ron Leake** Johnson County CC	**Randy Marak** Hill College	**George Marakas** University of Maryland
Charles Mattox, Jr. St. Mary's University	**Jim McCullough** Porter and Chester Institute	**Gail Miles** Lenoir-Rhyne College	**Steve Moore** University of South Florida
Anthony Nowakowski Buffalo State College	**John Passafiume** Clemson University	**Leonard Presby** William Paterson College	**Louis Pryor** Garland County CC
Michael Reilly University of Denver	**Dick Ricketts** Lane CC	**Dennis Santomauro** Kean College of New Jersey	**Pamela Schmidt** Oakton CC
Gary Schubert Alderson-Broaddus College	**T. Michael Smith** Austin CC	**Cynthia Thompson** Carl Sandburg College	**Marion Tucker** Northern Oklahoma College
JoAnn Weatherwax Saddleback College	**David Whitney** San Francisco State University	**James Wood** Tri-County Technical College	**Minnie Yen** University of Alaska Anchorage
Allen Zilbert Long Island University			

Contents

Overview

Over the past few years, the Internet has gradually become a household word. Advertisers, broadcasters, educators, magazines, and others routinely offer their Internet addresses as places to get more information on their products and services. For users of the Internet, those addresses are rapidly becoming more important than phone numbers. By the time you finish this course, you will understand why!

Objectives

After completing this Overview, you should be able to:

➤ **Understand some basic Internet concepts, issues, and terminology**

➤ **Understand the role of the World Wide Web in the Internet**

➤ **Identify the components of Netscape Communicator and the Internet tasks for which each is used**

➤ **Launch Netscape Communicator**

➤ **Identify parts of the Netscape Navigator 4.0 window and of the Communicator taskbar**

➤ **Customize the Netscape Navigator window**

➤ **Get online help for Netscape Communicator**

➤ **Exit Netscape Communicator**

What Is the Internet?

Today you cannot watch television, listen to the radio, or read a magazine or newspaper without encountering references to the Internet. In fact many magazines, newspapers, and television programs now publish their contents on the Internet. Imagine reading the daily newspaper or the latest edition of your favorite magazine on your computer screen. That concept may seem far-fetched, but it is reality. Many people are doing just that right now.

The Internet provides people with easier access to more information than has ever been possible before. From the Internal Revenue Service (IRS) and the Library of Congress to universities, businesses, and individuals just like you, it seems everyone is scrambling to publish and access information on the Internet. This situation can make the uninitiated a little tense when the word Internet comes up in conversation. Not to worry. If this course will be your first experience with the Internet, you will find it to be a much friendlier place to visit than did the Internet pioneers just a few years ago. You have chosen an ideal point in the evolution of this thing we call the Internet to get your feet wet. It has never been easier or more fun than it is today!

The Internet got its start in 1969 as **ARPAnet**, a computer network developed by the Advanced Research Projects Agency of the U.S. Department of Defense to ensure that the Defense Department computers could communicate with each other. For obvious reasons, the emphasis was to design a network over which information could travel even if certain network connections or computers in the network "died." So the robust, decentralized communication protocol (called **Internet Protocol**, or IP) which still exists today was first developed in the interest of U.S. national security.

For many years only government officials, and a few scientists and academics, had access to ARPAnet. The communication protocols developed for ARPAnet, however, were shared with the outside world, and it wasn't long before universities and other organizations began putting together their own IP-based networks. Then in the late 1980s the National Science Foundation, the National Aeronautics and Space Administration (NASA), and the Department of Energy provided funding that enabled IP-based networks to interconnect. This event gave rise to what we now know as the Internet—a collection of interconnected computer networks.

Remember all that talk about the Information Superhighway? Well in the last few years, government and (mostly) nongovernment money has been funding a massive communications line **backbone** for connecting major portions of the Internet in the United States. The idea is to create the analog for "freeways" on the Internet where there currently exists an immense tangle of "country roads." In addition, non-IP networks are currently connecting to the Internet via **gateways**, devices that connect networks whose communication protocols are different. So in the same way that ARPAnet and other IP-based networks have been absorbed into the Internet, other networks and computers of all kinds all over the world are rapidly becoming just another part of what we call the Internet.

How Does It Work?

The Internet is basically a collection of computers all over the world linked with telephonelike connections. If you have a computer at home with a **modem** (a device for modulating and demodulating digital signals for transmission over a regular telephone line), you know your computer can communicate with other computers over a telephone line. The communication is pretty slow, however, even with a fast modem. This is why the lines used for the Internet are much more powerful than those most of us have in our homes. These powerful lines are commonly referred to as ***digital lines***. They are provided by the telephone company just like regular phone lines and are increasingly easy to come by.

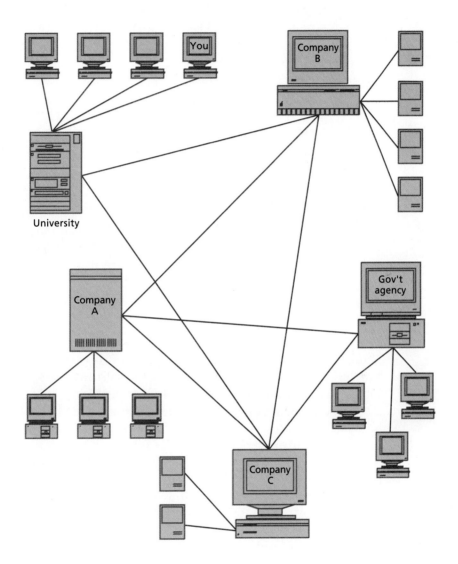

Stuart Harris and Gayle Kidder used a wonderful analogy in their book, *Netscape Quick Tour* (Ventana Press, Chapel Hill, 1995) for explaining how the Internet works. Here's our version. Imagine that the Internet is an immensely complex network of canals (instead of computers and communication lines). When anyone wants to send a message, they simply pop a message in a bottle, stick on an address label, walk to the nearest canal, and drop the bottle in the water. That's it. Except that your message must fit in the bottle. Messages too big to fit in one bottle must be divided between many bottles and thrown in the canal separately. There may be thousands of different routes your message could take to get to its destination, but the bottle (of course) has no knowledge of any of them—it's just bobbing along, taken wherever the current is headed.

Now imagine that at each canal junction there is a person with a net. This person, like each computer system on the Internet, knows which canals in the immediate area are blocked by barges, hopelessly clogged with bottles, or flowing relatively clearly. The person with the net fishes out all the bottles approaching the junction and checks the addresses. This person keeps bottles addressed to individuals who live around the junction and notifies those people by sending a messenger. The bottles addressed to other areas are thrown into a canal that is headed in generally the right direction and/or that is not blocked or clogged. This process is repeated every time a bottle approaches a junction, thereby ensuring that every bottle finally reaches its destination. None of the people at any canal junction knows anything about the condition of the network of canals beyond their immediate vicinity, and yet messages arrive at their destinations reliably.

This idea, that a network could function without someone somehow maintaining control over the entire network, was totally new when it was conceived in the late 1960s. It is the idea on which the entire Internet is based. It is the reason the Internet is a complex, disorganized, and often chaotic jumble of interconnectedness. It is also why the Internet works!

Who's the Boss?

The Internet of today belongs to no one. It is operated and administered by everyone involved. There is no one governing body, no board of directors, and no president. There are only shareholders—all those individuals, businesses, universities, governments, and other organizations that administer computers with access to the Internet. Each Internet participant has control only over its own computer or computer network. For example, you decide whether and when your home computer is connected to the Internet. Your school decides whether or not it will participate in the Internet; it also decides what information it will make available for public access and what information it will make available only to people with special passwords. Your school may set policies regarding what type of material is appropriate for Internet access on its own computers, but it cannot control the kind of information you access on other computers, say in Australia.

So the Internet is relatively disorganized and unregulated worldwide. It is feared by some governments as it represents an amazingly efficient way in which people with revolutionary ideas can disseminate information, communicate, and coordinate. The Internet is embraced by people in countries like the United States who seem to have an unquenchable thirst for information. This embrace may be conditional, however. There is a movement afoot to regulate the kind of information people in the United States may share via the Internet. Such regulation would require us to consider and define terms such as privacy, obscenity, and accessibility. These are words with which the United States government has grappled in its First Amendment interpretations for many decades.

The topic of Internet regulation is a particularly sticky one. The historical nature of the Internet has been one of open-mindedness and generosity. Computer administrators all over the world have done and continue to do their best to share as much information as possible. Individuals also play an important role in what you will find on the Internet. In fact, most of the material currently on the Internet was put there by the over 20 million individuals with Internet access. This means you will find information that amazes, bores, enlightens, confuses, enrages, offends, and delights you. The Internet is currently a gigantic worldwide public forum where absolutely anything goes. Lively discussions regarding whether or not this is wise, proper, safe, or appropriate promise to go on for years.

Of course, there is also a widespread and vocal movement to fight Internet regulation. In your travels on the Internet, you will sometimes encounter a blue ribbon. This symbol indicates support for free speech on the Internet.

What Is the World Wide Web?

The *World Wide Web* (often just called the Web) didn't exist prior to 1989. The Web is a very new and rapidly growing segment of the Internet developed for the sole purpose of making access to information on the Internet easier and faster. Back in the 1980s, when the Internet had made it possible to access hundreds of thousands of documents all over the world, the idea emerged of somehow linking documents in order to make related information easier to find.

Linked Documents

The idea of linking related documents is something like the age-old footnote or endnote. In books you sometimes encounter a word or phrase followed by a superscript number. This is one way of saying, "Look at the bottom of the page (or in the back of the book) for the corresponding number, and you will find more information about this." Instead of just referencing related documents as endnotes and footnotes often do, Web pages are actually linked to other documents using hypertext and, more recently, hypermedia links instead of footnotes.

Hypertext links allow you to click a highlighted word or phrase in one document and be instantly transported to the referenced document. This works because the clickable link actually contains information you cannot see about the exact location and name of another document. So when you click such a link, the referenced document is loaded and displayed on the screen. The referenced document might also contain hypertext links. So, by using these links, you are able to move through the Web in a literally weblike fashion by simply pointing and clicking. In just a few moments, you may travel the world, looking at documents residing on computers in North America, Europe, Australia, and beyond.

Hypermedia links go a step beyond hypertext in that they facilitate links using pictures, sounds, and movies in addition to text. Thanks to advances in microcomputer technology that allow the easy display of sound, motion video, and graphics, the Web has truly become multimedia.

What Is a Web Page?

So now you understand how documents on the Web are linked. But what are those documents? In its early days the Web was simply a new way of looking at the Internet rather than a new part of the Internet. The Web provided an easier way to view information that was already there. But as the idea of the Web caught on, special documents called ***Web pages*** began to proliferate. Unlike all other documents, Web pages are specifically designed to be accessed and displayed over the World Wide Web. Each Web page has a unique address called the ***Uniform Resource Locator (URL)*** which allows computers all over the world to locate it.

The term *page* was coined due to the similarity between the on-screen appearance of Web documents to the pages of a magazine. That is where the similarity ends, however. Unlike a magazine page, a Web page does not have a fixed-width, length, or physical location. In fact, a Web page is actually an encoded data document that can be read and interpreted by a Web browser like Netscape. The data document tells Netscape things like "place this picture here," "make this a header," "use this font and graphic here," and "link this text to this other Web page." Netscape uses the encoded information in the Web page data document to display the Web page itself. What you see on your screen is the actual Web page—an interpretation of a set of ***Hypertext Markup Language (HTML)*** instructions contained in a Web page data document.

That is all the casual Web user needs to know about the anatomy of Web pages. Because you are destined to become a fully qualified "Web surfer," however, you will learn a bit more about Web pages in this book.

What Are Web Browsers?

When the first strands of the Internet were strung together, the complex, command-line language used by the connected computers was the only way to access information on the Internet, and only a few academics, scientists, and military folks spoke that language with any fluency. Everyone else was to be summarily excluded from access to the increasing wealth of information available on the Internet until a friendlier method of Internet interaction was developed. The emergence of the Web was a step in the right direction. Its basic concept of document linking via hypertext would soon put an end to the necessity of laborious search and find operations. However, the Internet was still a cold and hostile environment for most of us. It was almost completely devoid of the user-friendly point-and-click interfaces that were quickly becoming the standard in so many other areas of human-computer interaction.

In 1993 the U.S. government designed an application to make the Web easily accessible and understandable, and a product called NCSA Mosaic emerged from the National Center for Supercomputing Applications (NCSA) in Illinois. (Interestingly, although Mosaic was a product of a U.S. government lab, it was actually designed almost entirely by undergraduates at the University of Illinois, Urbana-Champaign.) Mosaic was the first Windows-based *Web browser*, and it was received with tremendous enthusiasm by everyone interested in the Internet. Being a product of a U.S. government lab, it was also free, which was nice too.

The popularity and power of the Web browser did not escape the notice of alert entrepreneurs. Netscape Communications Corporation immediately hired the talented team of programmers who had developed Mosaic. Their marching orders were to design a bigger, better, more complete Web browser. The result was Netscape Navigator, and more recently, Netscape Communicator, a Web browser application which has evolved into a collection of tightly coupled applications used to make the most of the Internet for business and communication.

Hot on the heels of Netscape has come a host of other Web browsing tools including Netscape's arch rival, Microsoft, with Explorer. Netscape's tools, however, have become overwhelmingly popular, perhaps even the de facto standard, for harnessing the power of the Internet. It is for this reason that you will be using Netscape Communicator for the Internet projects in this book.

Tip While life holds few guarantees, the Internet, and therefore the World Wide Web, offers one guarantee: Nothing ever stays the same! Although we have done our best to provide the most current view of Internet and Web locations referenced in this book, it is almost a certainty that there will have been changes by the time you read this module. Don't worry if the screen sometimes looks different from the figures in this text. Remember, the Internet is constantly changing!

Introducing Netscape Communicator

As already discussed, Netscape's first Internet product was a Web browser called Navigator. Navigator has evolved over the years into its current incarnation, **Netscape Communicator**, of which Navigator 4.0 is just one component. Netscape Communicator is a product composed of several tightly integrated components designed to provide a rich and complete set of services for today's Web users.

The five basic components of Netscape Communicator and the primary functions of each are as follows:

Netscape Navigator 4.0 is a Web browser tool. It is the cornerstone of Communicator's ability to access and display the wealth of information available on the Internet and the Web.

Netscape Messenger is the electronic mail (e-mail) component of Netscape Communicator. *E-mail* refers to specially addressed electronic messages which are sent and received over the Internet. Netscape Messenger has a number of powerful features increasing the effectiveness of e-mail. Among these features is allowing users to take advantage of the rich content of the Web for e-mail messages.

Netscape Collabra is the Communicator component designed to provide access to Internet newsgroups, electronic discussion forums. Collabra goes beyond the traditional role of news browser, though, and provides valuable information sharing features.

Netscape Composer was formerly the cornerstone of Netscape Navigator Gold, a Web authoring tool. Composer has now been moved into the core Netscape Communicator product, allowing users to easily create richly formatted Internet documents.

Netscape Conference is a real-time audio and data collaboration tool. With Conference, users can conduct *fully duplex* (in which you speak and listen simultaneously) Internet telephone calls, send *voice mail* (an electronically stored voice message) over the Internet, and share data.

You will be using these Netscape Communicator components as you work your way through the projects in this book.

If You've Used Previous Versions of Navigator...

Communicator will look familiar if you've used previous versions of Navigator—familiar yet different. The primary difference is the idea that the Communicator product has been broken into components. For example, previous versions of Navigator included e-mail and newsgroup facilities. Now Navigator is purely a Web browser, and Communicator's Messenger and Collabra components are dedicated to e-mail and newsgroups. In addition, where Navigator Gold included Web *authoring* tools (tools for creating Web pages), Composer is a dedicated Communicator component dedicated to Web authoring.

While Communicator is now composed of a number of components, these components are by no means *"stand-alone"*—you cannot install just one of them; they come as an integrated set. In fact, the components of Communicator are tightly intergrated. For example, the address book is shared by Messenger, Collabra, and Conference. The Web authoring facilities of Composer are shared with Messenger and Collabra for rich e-mail and newsgroup message *formatting* (specifying the way in which you want Web browsers to display messages you compose).

If you've used previous versions of Navigator, you will notice the Communicator task bar as something new. The task bar is a short cut for navigating between Communicator components. The toolbars have undergone some changes, but will look familiar.

Most noteworthy of the changes between previous versions of Navigator and Communicator is expanded functionality. Tools like spell checking and rich formatting for e-mail and newsgroups is just the start. Communicator includes Conference, a component which offers a host of cool ways to communicate and collaborate over the Internet. Composer allows you to easily author your own Web pages. The list goes on. For now, if you've used a previous version of Navigator, you have a leg up on the current product. But pay attention, because a lot has changed!

Launching Communicator

In this book we assume you are using a computer running Windows95. If you are using WindowsNT or another type of computer like a Macintosh or a UNIX workstation, your procedure for starting up the Netscape Communicator program will be different than the one presented here. It is important to note, however, that Netscape Communicator is designed to look and feel the same on any computer platform. This means that if you are using Netscape Communicator in an environment other than Windows95, you can still use most of the material in this book.

To get started with Netscape Communicator, you will launch Netscape Navigator 4.0. Remember that Navigator is a Web browser and is the cornerstone of the Communicator product. It is a natural place to start when beginning your exploration of Communicator.

Tip The following instructions for starting Netscape Communicator may not be appropriate for your school. For example, you may have a Netscape Communicator Shortcut icon on your Windows 95 desktop, or the Start menu may be organized differently than the one shown. Ask your instructor if you need help launching Communicator.

TASK 1: TO LAUNCH NETSCAPE COMMUNICATOR

1 Click the Start button **Start** and point to Programs.

2 Point to the Netscape Communicator folder and then click Netscape Navigator in the pull-down menus.

The Netscape Navigator 4.0 program is launched.

The Netscape Communicator startup screen appears and remains on your screen while your computer establishes its connection to the network.

The startup screen disappears when a network connection has been confirmed. It is replaced by the Netscape Navigator window and the Communicator taskbar.

Identifying Parts of the Navigator Window

The Netscape Navigator 4.0 window is much like those of other Windows applications. It contains a title bar, menu bar, toolbars, and scroll bars. These are features you will find in nearly all Windows applications. The Netscape window also has an area where documents are displayed, a location field, a progress bar, and a status indicator.

Location field: shows the address of the currently displayed page, and allows you to enter the address of an Internet document to view.

Location toolbar: provides tools for bookmarking and jumping to specific locations on the Web.

Menu bar: gives you point-and-click access to Netscape commands.

Navigation toolbar: provides buttons for navigating the Web.

Page display area: displays the content of an Internet document or Web page. Text, graphics, and other displayed content can be selected and copied. Sometimes the page display is divided into rectangular frames, each containing its own page content.

Personal toolbar: a customizable toolbar which allows you to set up short cuts to your favorite Web sites.

Progress bar: gives information about Netscape's progress in transferring Internet documents to your computer and/or a description of on-screen activity.

Scroll bar: gives you a way to move around in the currently displayed Web page or document.

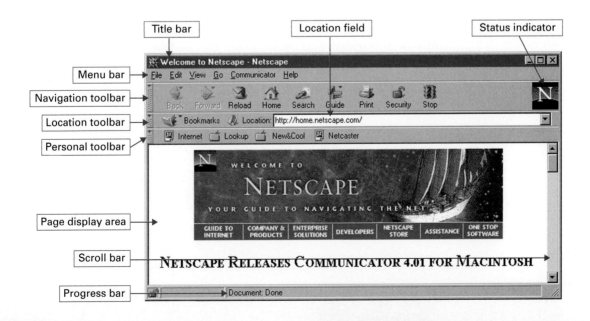

Status indicator: indicates Netscape's current status by displaying animated shooting stars when a transfer is in progress. You can click the status indicator to go to Netscape's home page.

Title bar: contains the title of the application (Netscape) and the document file you are currently viewing (for example, *Welcome to Netscape* or the name of your school's home page).

Understanding the Component Bar

Below the Netscape Navigator window, or in the lower right corner, you will see the component bar. This **component bar** is designed to give you quick access to the most commonly used Communicator components.

The component bar can be used as a floating palette, displayed separately from the active Communicator window.

The component bar can also be "docked" in the lower right corner of the active Communicator window by clicking the Windows95 close box in the upper right corner of the taskbar. When it's docked, you can "undock" the component bar by clicking the "handle" on the left end of the component bar.

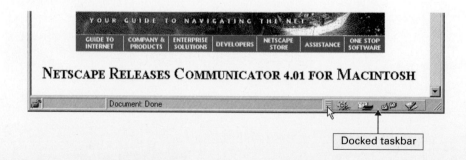

Docked taskbar

The component bar contains four buttons, each of which accesses frequently used Communicator components. You can point to each icon for a description of the component accessed by that button.

The first button, a ship's wheel, accesses Communicator's Web browser, Netscape Navigator 4.0.

The second button accesses your e-mail inbox in Netscape Messenger.

The third button accesses Internet discussion groups using Netscape Collabra.

Finally, the last button accesses Communicator's Web authoring tool, Netscape Composer.

Customizing the Navigator Window

You can customize Netscape's appearance on your screen to suit your own preferences. The toolbars and location field can be hidden and moved. You can also change screen colors and fonts.

TASK 2: TO HIDE TOOLBARS

 Point to the handle on the left side of the Personal toolbar.

Notice that the handle is highlighted.

2 Click the handle, and the toolbar disappears, replaced by a clickable tab.

You can restore the hidden toolbar by simply clicking the tab.

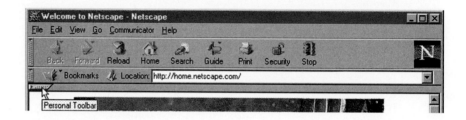

You can also use Netscape's View menu to hide and show selected toolbars.

TASK 3: TO REARRANGE TOOLBARS

1 Point to the handle on the left side of the Location toolbar.

2 Drag the Location toolbar upward.

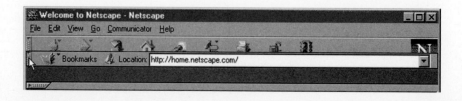

3 Drop the Location toolbar.

Notice that the Location toolbar is now at the top with the Navigation toolbar below it.

You can move the Location toolbar back to its original position by dragging it downward in the same way.

TASK 4: TO CHANGE DISPLAY COLORS

1 Choose Preferences from the Edit menu.

The Preferences window appears displaying the Navigator preferences screen.

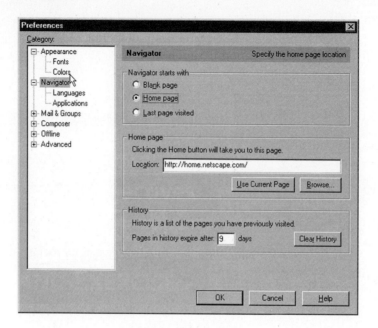

2   Select Colors from the tree menu.

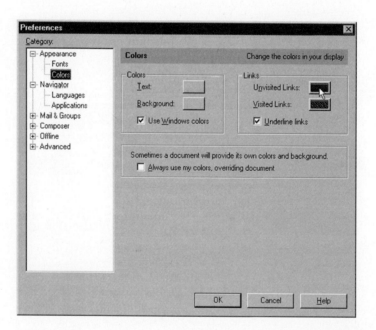

Notice that the current display colors are shown in the Colors Preferences screen. From this screen you can select your own color preferences for links, text, and the background of Web pages. Links are discussed in detail in Project 1. For now, all you need to know is that links are special text on

Web pages that are usually displayed in a different color from regular text so that they are easy to spot.

3 Select the color button for either visited or unvisited Links on the Colors Preferences screen.

The colors from which you may choose are displayed in the Color palette. Notice this palette also allows you to define your own custom colors using the Define Custom Colors button.

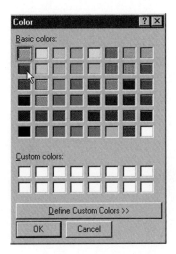

4 Select a color from the Basic Colors palette.

5 Select the ` OK ` button on the Color palette.

Notice that the color you selected is now displayed for Links on the Color Preferences screen. Repeat steps 3 through 5 to change the selected color again.

Note Many Web pages have predefined colors that will override your color selections.

6 Select the box labeled "Always use my colors, overriding document" to make sure color changes you make will be displayed on the current document.

7 Select the ` OK ` button on the Colors Preferences screen.

Can you find the links on the currently displayed document? They now appear in the color you selected. Use the vertical scroll bar to view the entire document if necessary.

8 Repeat these steps to select new colors for each of the remaining screen parts. Remember to choose colors that contrast well with the document background and that are easy on the eyes.

TASK 5: TO CHANGE FONTS

1 Choose Preferences from the Edit menu.

The Preferences window appears displaying the Navigator Preferences screen.

2 Select Fonts from the tree menu.

The current display fonts are shown on the Fonts Preferences screen. From this screen you can select your own font preferences for text that Netscape will display in a variable-width font and for text that Netscape will display in a fixed-width font.

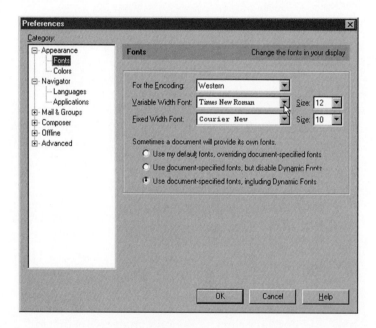

3 Select the down-arrow button to the right of the variable-width Font field.

The fonts from which you may choose to use for the display of variable-width font text are displayed in a pull-down menu (***variable-width fonts*** are ones in which different letters occupy different amounts of horizontal space.). Notice that you can select both the font and the size.

4 Select a new font from the menu of fonts displayed.

5 Select the OK button on the Fonts Preferences screen.

How does the currently displayed document look? Use the vertical scroll bar to view the entire document if necessary. Repeat these steps to experiment with the font setting until you find a font and size that looks nice on the screen and is easy to read.

> **Tip** 12-point Times is a popular choice for the variable width font, and 12-point Courier is often selected as a fixed width font (***Fixed width fonts*** are ones in which all characters occupy a fixed amount of horizontal space.). Both of these fonts are available on most computers.

Getting Online Help

Like most other Windows applications, Netscape offers a Help menu to assist you with questions or problems that may arise while you learn to use the application. Unlike other Windows applications, however, many of Netscape's help facilities are available ***online***—over the Internet. While the meaning of online help is hotly contested, in this context it means that many help screens provided by Netscape are actually Web pages located on some other computer which you access over the Internet, online. The advantage to offering this type of online help is that Netscape Corporation can continuously update the available information. For example, it can post answers to questions frequently asked by users.

TASK 6: TO ACCESS ONLINE HELP

1 Choose Help from the menu bar.

A number of options appear in the Help menu. The one you will probably find most useful is Help Contents.

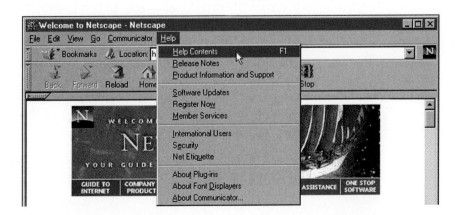

2 Choose the Help Contents option.

Netscape takes you to the Netscape Communicator online help screen.

3 Use the scroll bars to view the entire page.

From the Netscape Communicator online help page you can access information about any text displayed as colored text links. (Remember your color selections?) Simply click a link, and Netscape takes you to the Web page that covers that topic.

4 Explore Netscape Communicator online help by clicking links that interest you. Try clicking the Communicator components displayed.

5 Click the close button or choose Close from the command menu to close the online help window when you have finished exploring.

Exiting Communicator

Most Windows application use the same command to exit, so if you have used any other Windows applications, you already know how to exit Netscape Communicator.

TASK 7: TO EXIT NETSCAPE COMMUNICATOR

 Choose Exit from the File menu.

The Conclusion

You can either take a well-deserved break, or you can work on the Review Exercises and Assignments.

22

Summary and Exercises

Summary

- The Internet is a collection of computers all over the world interconnected by powerful telephonelike lines called digital lines.
- The Internet began as ARPAnet, a U.S. Defense Department project initiated in the late 1960s.
- Although there is discussion in the country regarding regulating some aspects of the Internet, there is no one organization in charge of the Internet.
- The architecture of the Internet is completely decentralized,.
- The Web is the newest, fastest growing segment of the Internet.
- The Web was developed to make accessing information on the Internet easier.
- A Web page is a special document designed specifically to be displayed by a Web browser like Netscape Navigator.
- Web pages are created using Hypertext Markup Language (HTML).
- The location of Web pages on the Internet is designated by the Uniform Resource Locator (URL), a unique standardized address.
- Netscape Communicator is a collection of tightly coupled tools for Web users.
- Netscape Navigator 4.0 is a component of Netscape Communicator. It is a Web browser application designed to display Web pages and to provide an easy-to-use interface for navigating the Internet.
- The Internet is constantly changing.
- You can modify the appearance of the Netscape Navigator window by hiding and rearranging toolbars and by selecting display fonts and colors.
- You can access online help in Netscape Communicator using the Help menu.

Key Terms and Operations

Key Terms
ARPAnet
backbone
component bar
digital line
e-mail
fixed-width fonts
formatting
fully duplex
gateway
hypermedia links
hypertext links
Hypertext Markup Language (HTML)
Internet
Internet Protocol (IP)
location field
menu bar
modem
Netscape Collabra
Netscape Communicator
Netscape Composer
Netscape Conference

Operations
launch Netscape Communicator
display General Preferences
set Font and Color Preferences
hide and rearrange toolbars
access Online Help
exit Netscape Communicator

Netscape Messenger
Netscape Navigator 4.0
progress bar
online
page display area
scroll bar
stand-alone
status indicator
title bar
toolbar
Uniform Resource Locator (URL)
variable-width fonts
voice mail
Web authoring
Web browser
Web page
World Wide Web

Study Questions

Multiple Choice

1. The World Wide Web is a segment of the Internet that
   a. allows related documents to be linked.
   b. is constantly changing.
   c. makes accessing information on the Internet easier.
   d. All of the above.

2. On a Web page a hypertext link is a
   a. program used to download text files from the Internet.
   b. pointer to a related Internet document.
   c. very fast text editor.
   d. connection between two words.

3. When the Internet first started out, it was called
   a. WorldNet.
   b. DECnet.
   c. ARPAnet.
   d. Mosaic.

4. The Internet is controlled entirely by
   a. the U.S. Defense Department.
   b. an elected board of directors.
   c. the National Science Foundation.
   d. no one.

5. Netscape Navigator 4.0 is an application called a
   a. Web cruiser.
   b. Net crawler.
   c. Web browser.
   d. None of the above.

Short Answer

1. The _____ at the bottom of the Netscape window gives information about Netscape's current status.

2. A URL is a unique _____ used to locate documents on the Web.

3. The Internet is constantly _____.

4. The _____ is the most recent segment of the Internet to arise and the fastest growing.

5. The Information Superhighway is a term used for the powerful communications lines or _____ being developed to increase the speed and efficiency of the Internet in the United States.

For Discussion

1. Should there be a governing body overseeing the Internet and setting policies, standards, and rules? Why? Why not?

2. What are three aspects of the Netscape Navigator 4.0 window that you have learned to customize?

Getting Started with Netscape Navigator 4.0

Using Navigator's Navigation toolbar, history feature, and location field for getting around on the Web and using bookmarks for organizing your travels on the Web are all important skills to learn before going further with your exploration of the Internet.

Objectives

After completing this project, you will be able to:

➤ **Use Netscape Navigator 4.0 navigational buttons**

➤ **Navigate using links**

➤ **Revisit sites using the history feature**

➤ **Print a Web page**

➤ **Create, delete, and organize bookmarks**

The Challenge

Assume you are finishing your undergraduate degree and are preparing to enter the job market following graduation. You have consulted the placement services office at your school and are convinced that there must be more job opportunities in your field than those you found there. When you ask if there are other sources you might consult for employment opportunities in your field, a placement services representative suggests you try the World Wide Web.

Intrigued, you asked what advantages the World Wide Web might offer. You learn that information available on the Web may be more complete and will almost certainly be more timely than almost any other source. You have heard others refer to the Web as an apparently inexhaustible source of information and are anxious to give it a try, especially if it will provide up-to-the-minute information about employers who are hiring in your field.

The Solution

In this Project you will gain the important skills of getting around on the Web and returning to Web locations you have already visited using Netscape Navigator 4.0. Getting your feet wet with Netscape Navigator is the first step in accessing resources on the Internet and the World Wide Web for use in your job search.

Navigating Using Netscape Navigator 4.0

Before you can begin exploring the Web, you must first start your Web browser, Netscape Navigator 4.0, the cornerstone component of Netscape Communicator. This procedure is covered in the Overview if you need a refresher.

With Navigator open take a look at the Navigation Toolbar located just below the menu bar. Navigator's command toolbar is a set of icons you can use to perform commonly used functions. The toolbar contains some of the tools you will need to navigate from one Web site to another. These navigational tools are Back, Forward, and Home. In this section you will use each of these navigational buttons and learn how they can help you to get around on the Web.

Finding Yourself on the Web

When you start Netscape Navigator 4.0, you are dropped off somewhere on the Web. You may find yourself delivered to the Welcome to Netscape page, or you might be looking at your school's **home page** (the "front door" to a Web site). The Web location where Navigator goes upon startup is often referred to as the startup location and is determined by the specific Navigator setup you are using. The address of your current location on the Web is displayed in the location field just below the Navigation toolbar.

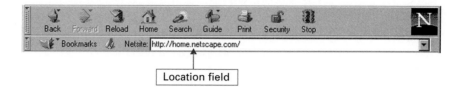

The address displayed in the location field is in a standard format and is called the Uniform Resource Locator (URL). URLs can be quite long and may seem complicated. Actually, the standard format of URLs makes them fairly easy to understand. URLs are composed of three parts: *protocol, domain name,* and *file name.*

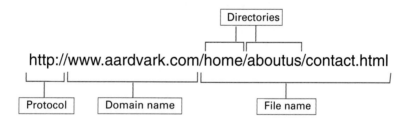

Take a look at the URL displayed in the location field on your screen. The **protocol** is the part of the address preceding the two forward slashes. The protocol designates the type of Internet document and allows your Web browser to interpret the information in the document appropriately for correct display on your screen. In the example above, the protocol is http: (for Hypertext Transfer Protocol) which indicates the document is a Web page created using the universal Web page authoring language called HTML (for Hypertext Markup Language).

The **domain name** is the part after the two forward slashes and before the next slash. It designates the computer or server on which the file is located. In the example above, the complete domain name is www.aardvark.com.

The first part of this particular domain name, "www", indicates a particular computer or server within the aardvark.com domain on which the given Web document resides. The prefix "www" is often used on the Web to indicate that the address points to a Web server. You will also see other prefixes, like "ftp," "gopher," and "home". These are all simply the names of computers within a given domain.

The suffix "com" indicates that the domain name belongs to a company. (Other domain name suffixes you will often see include .edu for educational institutions, .net for Internet service providers, .org for nonprofit organizations, and .gov for governmental agencies.)

Generally, the portion of the domain name immediately preceding the suffix is used to help us identify the owner of the domain name at a glance. In this case we are talking about the portion of the domain name that reads "aardvark." A good guess might be that this domain belongs to a company called Aardvark. Real-life examples of company domain names include netscape.com (Netscape Corp.), apple.com (Apple Computer), and cnn.com (CNN). In fact, domain names are so frequently simply company names that you can often find a company's Web site by guessing its domain name!

Note You will encounter many domain names on the Internet that are simply the names of companies and organizations. In fact, the purpose of domain names was originally to "humanize" the complex numbering system used to uniquely identify each computer on the Internet. But so many domain names have now been registered that you will often find companies using rather contrived or non-intuitive domain names. Why? Because the one they wanted was taken!

The *file name* is everything after the slash following the domain name. The file name specifies the local directory path and file name of an Internet document. In the previous example, the file name is "/home/aboutus/contact.html." This means that the Web page file called "contact.html" is located inside a directory called "aboutus" which is located inside a directory called "home."

Let's look at another example of a URL by exploring the Welcome to Netscape page a bit.

Note If the Welcome to Netscape page is not currently displayed on your screen, click the status indicator in the Navigator window.

Move your mouse pointer over the button labeled Assistance below the Netscape logo. Watch the Progress bar at the bottom of your screen. As your mouse passes over the Assistance button.

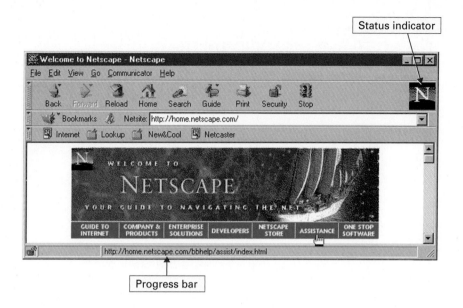

The following URL appears in the progress bar: http://home.netscape.com /bbhelp/assist/index.html. The file name portion of this URL is everything after the domain name: /bbhelp/assist/index.html. This file name indicates that a file named "index.html" is located in a directory called "assist" that is inside a directory called "bbhelp" that resides on the Netscape computer whose domain name is "home.netscape.com."

Note Unlike **MS-DOS** (a disk operating system used on IBM compatible personal computers), directory paths which use backward slashes (\) to delineate directories, URLs employ forward slashes (/) or uphill slashes. This is because the URL is written for the UNIX operating system, and UNIX uses forward slashes to delineate directories in directory paths. Notice also that file names in URLs are often longer than the standard DOS format. This can also be blamed on UNIX which allows file and directory names to be long enough to be meaningful!

Going Places Using URLs

There are many ways to jump from one Web page to another. If you know the URL of the location you'd like to visit, the quickest way to get there is by using that address.

30

TASK 1: TO USE THE LOCATION FIELD

1   Click the location field, and completely select the URL displayed.

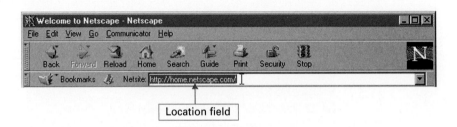

Location field

2   Type the following URL in the location field:
http://home.netscape.com/home/internet-search.html

Notice that when you type in the location field, its label changes to Go to, indicating that the site you are typing is the site you want to visit.

3   Press (ENTER)

Navigator will attempt to connect to the host specified in the URL (home.netscape.com). If successful, Navigator will open the file you specified in the path (home/internet-search.html), using the given protocol (http:). Watch the progress bar at the bottom of the Navigator window to see what Navigator is up to. You will see messages like "Connect," "Contacting host," "Transferring data," "Waiting for reply," and "Reading file" flash by as the document you requested is located and prepared for display on your screen. If all goes well, you will soon find yourself looking at the Netscape Net Search page.

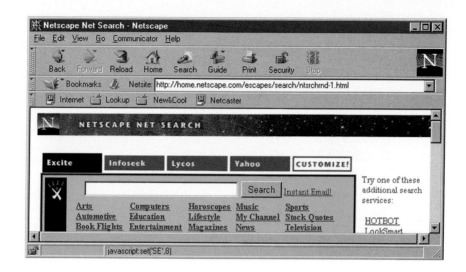

Don't Panic if your screen doesn't look just like the one shown above. Remember, the Web is constantly changing, and it's very likely the Net Search page has changed in the short time since this module was printed.

TASK 2: TO GO FURTHER WITH THE LOCATION FIELD

1 Click the location field, and again completely select the URL displayed.

2 Type the following URL in the location field: **http://wsj.com**

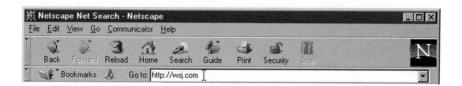

3 Press (ENTER)

Navigator once again takes you to the Web page specified in the URL you entered. This time the address you entered is for the Wall Street Journal Interactive Edition home page.

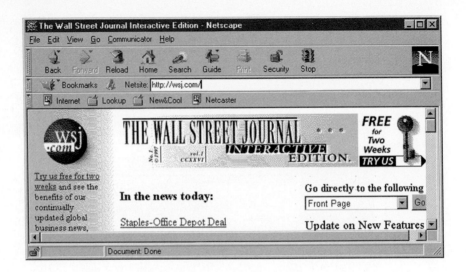

Going Places You've Already Been

When visiting locations on the Web, you may want to return to places you have already been. That is where the Back button comes in. The Back button allows you to retrace your steps through the Web. Each time you choose it, the Back button takes you to the Web page you were visiting immediately before the one currently displayed on the screen.

Your travels through the Web so far are illustrated below. You can use this illustration to help you understand the navigational tools demonstrated in this section.

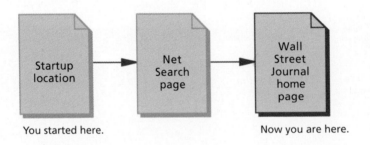

You started here.   Now you are here.

TASK 3: TO USE THE BACK BUTTON

1   Select ![Back] from the Navigation toolbar.

2   Select ![Back] again.

Navigator takes you back to the startup page where you began.

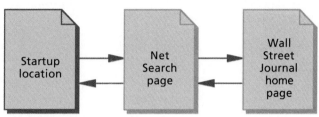

Now you are here.

Whenever you retrace your steps using the Back button, you can then use the Forward button to return to pages from which you've backed up. You just used the Back button to go from the Wall Street Journal page to the Net Search page to the startup location, which is where you are now. What will happen if you now select the Forward button?

TASK 4: TO USE THE FORWARD BUTTON

1 Select ![Forward] from the Navigation toolbar.

You are returned to the Web page from which you last backed up: the Net Search page.

2 Select ![Forward] again.

Navigator takes you forward again to the Wall Street Journal home page. Notice that the Forward button is no longer available. This means you have reached the farthest forward point in your Web travels so far.

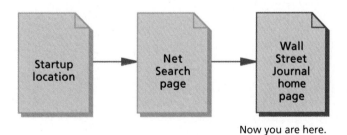

Now you are here.

Tip There are other ways to go back and forward. You can choose Back and Forward from the Go menu. You can press (ALT) + ← (Back) and (ALT) + → (Forward). Finally, you can click the right mouse button for a small dialog box containing the options Back and Forward.

34

After you visit a number of Web sites, getting back to your starting point using the Back button can become tedious. The Home button allows you to return to the startup location in one easy step.

TASK 5: TO GO HOME

1 Select from the Navigator toolbar.

You are returned to the Web page from which you started.

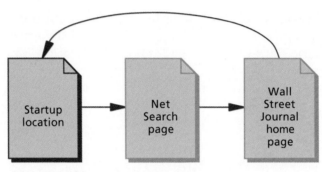

Now you are home.

> **Tip** You can also go home by selecting Home from the Go menu.

Navigator offers another feature to help you revisit Web locations and keep track of where you've been. This feature is called **history.** As you may have already guessed, for the Back and Forward buttons to work, Navigator must keep track of where you go.

TASK 6: TO USE THE HISTORY FEATURE

1 Choose Go from the menu bar.

Notice that all the locations you have visited during this session are listed as options on the Go menu. The checked location is the one currently displayed on the screen.

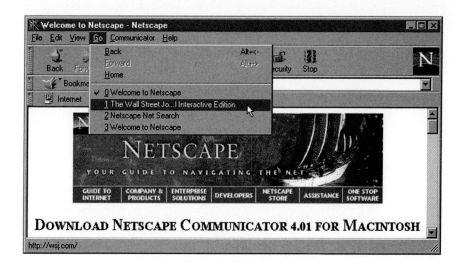

2 Choose the Wall Street Journal Interactive Edition option, or type the number corresponding to the Wall Street Journal menu option.

Navigator takes you directly to the Wall Street Journal home page.

Navigating Using Links

So far you've learned how to use some of Navigator's features for navigating between Web pages. Recall, though, that the single most powerful feature of the World Wide Web is the use of linked documents. In this section you will learn to identify links on Web pages and to use them for navigating the Web.

Finding Links on Web Pages

Most Web pages contain *links* to other Web pages. **Links** can be text or pictures appearing on a Web page, and Navigator makes it easy to identify them. Depending on the specific Navigator setup you are using, ***text links*** appear in a different color, or underlined, or both. ***Picture links*** can be identified by moving the cursor around on the screen. When you pass over either a text or picture link, the cursor icon changes to a hand (🖑). Finally, when the cursor is on a link, the URL of the linked document appears in the progress bar.

On the Wall Street Journal page (next page), the cursor is positioned over a picture link. Notice that the cursor icon has become a hand and the URL of the linked document appears in the progress bar.

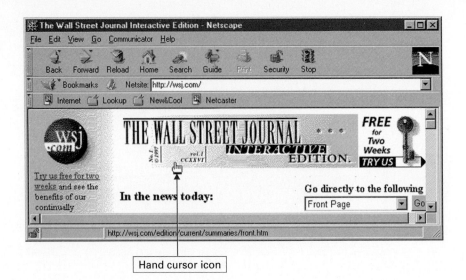

Hand cursor icon

TASK 7: TO LOCATE LINKS

1　If you are not already there, go to the Net Search page. You can select on the Navigation toolbar, or you can use the Go menu.

2　Move the pointer around on the Net Search page. Locate picture and text links by looking for colored or underlined text and watching for the hand icon that appears when you find a link. Use the scroll bars to display the entire page if necessary.

Don't Panic　If you click any of the links you find and are transported away from the Net Search page, remember you can use the Back button or the Go menu to get back to where you were before.

Going Places Using Links

Now that you know how to find links on Web pages, it's time to start using links to get around.

TASK 8: TO SELECT A LINK

1　Go to the Net Search page, if you're not already there.

2　Position the cursor over the Yahoo! picture link, as shown on the previous page.

Notice the URL that appears in the status bar. This is the address of the linked document to which you will jump when you select the link.

3 Select the picture link by clicking it.

You are transported to a special Net Search page featuring Yahoo! This page provides a direct interface with Yahoo!, a popular tool for performing searches on the Internet.

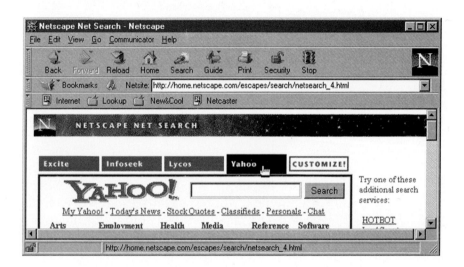

Printing Web Pages

Once you have arrived at a Web page that contains valuable information, you may wish to print that page. Navigator offers standard Preview and Print functions, making printing Web pages in Navigator very much like printing documents in other Windows applications.

TASK 9: TO USE PRINT PREVIEW

1 Type the following URL in the location field:
http://www.collegegrad.com

2 Press (ENTER)

The College Grad Job Hunter page appears.

3 Choose Print Preview from the File menu.

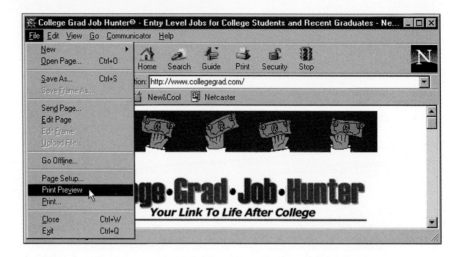

The current Web page is displayed in a print preview window. Notice the buttons along the top of the window. You can use these buttons to print the page, view the next printed page (remember, Web pages can be very long!), view two pages side-by-side, zoom in for a closer look, zoom out, or close the print preview window.

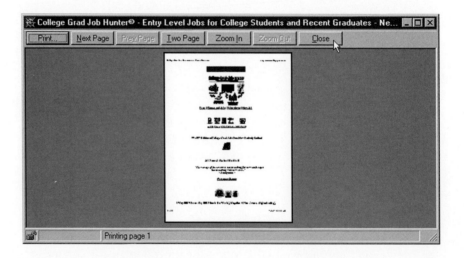

4 Select [Close]

The File menu also offers a Page Setup option which allows you to make changes to the way the current page is printed. When selected, the Print Setup option displays the Page Setup screen. Using the Page Setup screen, you can modify print options such as margins, headers, and footers.

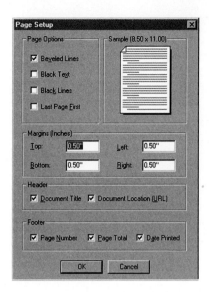

TASK 10: TO USE THE PRINT OPTION

1   Choose Print from the File menu.

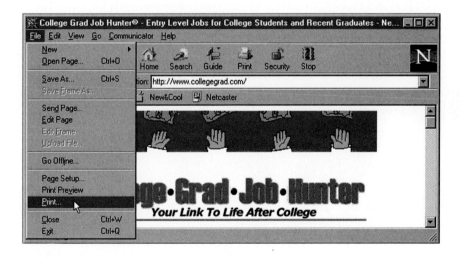

> **Tip**   Another way to use the print function in Navigator is to select the Print button on the Navigation toolbar.

The Print window appears. The Print window allows you to specify which pages you wish to print, the print quality, the number of copies, and whether or not you wish to have multiple copies collated.

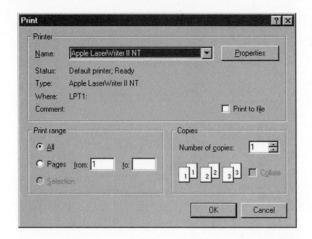

2 Make any changes you wish to the print options displayed.

3 Select OK

The College Grad Job Hunter page is printed on your computer's default printer.

Using Bookmarks

Bookmarks provide a way for you to make a permanent record of the addresses (URLs) of your favorite Web pages or of Web sites you would like to remember and perhaps visit again sometime in the future. Navigator bookmarks include the name of the site, its URL, the date you "marked" the site, and the last time you visited the site. Unlike the history feature, bookmarks persist from one Navigator session to another and do not disappear unless you manually delete them.

Creating Bookmarks

Unlike Navigator's history feature, which automatically records sites you have visited during the current session, bookmarks must be created manually. To create a bookmark for the currently displayed Web page, you can use the Bookmarks menu.

TASK 11: TO CREATE BOOKMARKS USING THE BOOKMARKS MENU

1 If you're not already there, go to the College Grad Job Hunter page at http://www.collegegrad.com

2 Click the Bookmark QuickFile button Bookmarks on the location toolbar.

3   Select Add Bookmark from the Bookmark QuickFile menu.

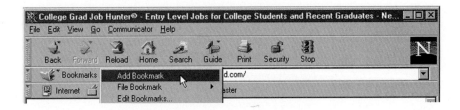

You have just created a bookmark for the College Grad Job Hunter page.

> **Tip** To create a bookmark for the currently displayed document, you can also use the Communicator menu: Choose Bookmarks, and then Add Bookmark. The keyboard shortcut to create a bookmark for the currently displayed page is CTRL + D

4   Click the Bookmark QuickFile button   Bookmarks   on the location toolbar.

Notice that College Grad Job Hunter is now displayed in the Bookmark QuickFile menu. Each time you create a bookmark, it will be added to this list in the Bookmark QuickFile menu. When you want to return to a Web site you have bookmarked, you simply select that site in this menu, and Navigator will take you directly there.

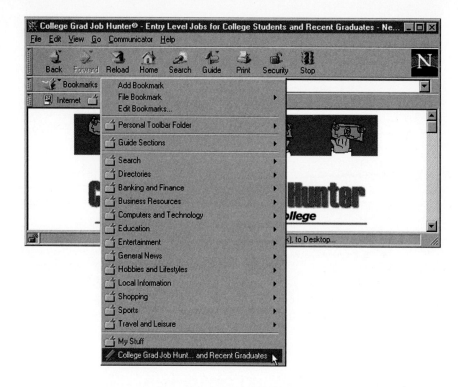

Deleting Bookmarks

Because the World Wide Web is always changing, so must your list of bookmarks. Pages will change and even disappear over time. Or, if a particular marked Web page persists long enough, your interests may change, and you may wish to remove it from your list of bookmarks. For these reasons, it is important to be able to delete bookmarks.

TASK 12: TO DELETE A BOOKMARK

1 Choose Edit Bookmarks from the Bookmark QuickFile menu.

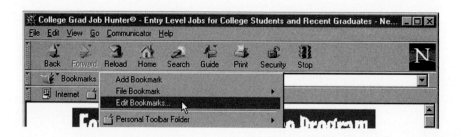

The Bookmarks window appears.

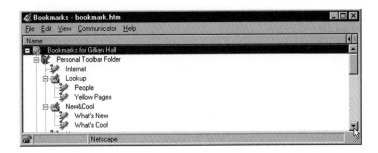

2   Scroll down to view your new bookmark.

3   Select the College Grad Job Hunter bookmark.

4   Choose Delete from the Bookmarks window Edit menu.

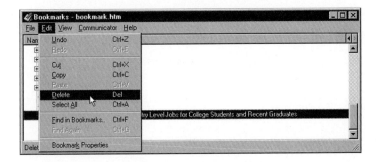

The bookmark disappears from the Bookmarks window and also from the Bookmarks menu.

> **Tip** You can also delete a bookmark from the Bookmarks window by selecting it and pressing `DEL`

5   Choose Undo from the Bookmarks window Edit menu to undelete the bookmark.

Notice that the College Grad bookmark is restored in both the Bookmarks window and in the Bookmark QuickFile menu.

Organizing Bookmarks

As you have seen, bookmarks you create are displayed in both the Bookmarks menu and the Bookmarks window. As you become an active Web surfer, you will soon find yourself accumulating large numbers of bookmarks, and you may wish to organize them into categories to make them easier to find. Navigator provides folders for just this kind of organizing. *Folders* are used to group bookmarks into categories that you define.

TASK 13: TO CREATE A BOOKMARK FOLDER

1 If the Bookmarks window is not already open, choose Edit Bookmarks from the Bookmark QuickFile menu.

The Bookmarks window appears.

2 Choose New Folder from the Bookmarks window File menu.

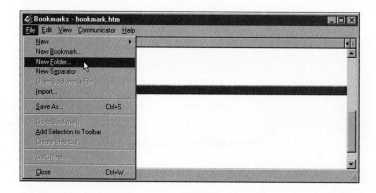

The Bookmark Properties window appears.

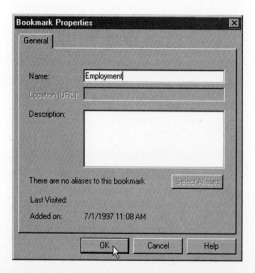

3 Type **Employment** in the Name field.

4 Select [OK]

A folder called Employment has been added to the Bookmarks window. This new bookmarks folder does not contain any bookmarks yet. The next step is to move a bookmark into the folder.

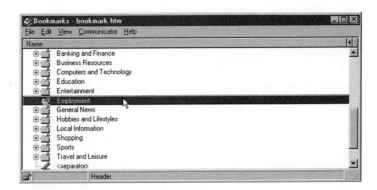

TASK 14: TO MOVE BOOKMARKS INTO A FOLDER

1 Select the College Grad Job Hunter bookmark in the Bookmarks window, and drag it to the Employment folder.

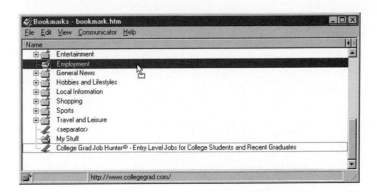

Notice that the College Grad Job Hunter bookmark is now indented beneath the Employment folder. This means that it is now inside the folder.

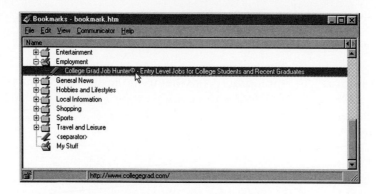

2   Close the Bookmarks window.

3   Click the Bookmark QuickFile button [🖋 Bookmarks] on the location toolbar.

Notice that the Employment folder appears in the Bookmark QuickFile menu.

4   Select the Employment folder.

A submenu appears containing the College Grad Job Hunter bookmark.

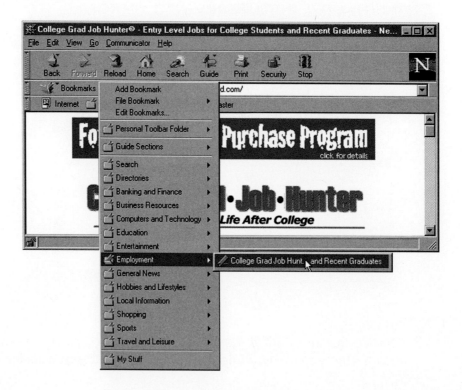

TASK 15: TO DELETE A BOOKMARK FOLDER

1 Select Edit Bookmarks from the Bookmark QuickFile menu.

2 Select the Employment folder in the Bookmarks window.

3 Choose Delete from the Bookmarks window Edit menu, or simply press
(DEL)

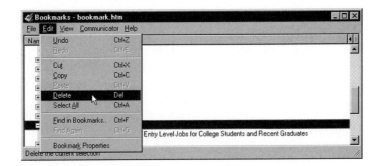

The Employment folder disappears.

4 Choose Undo from the Bookmarks window Edit menu.

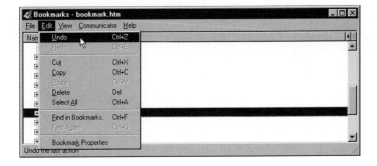

The Employment folder is restored in the Bookmarks window.

5 Close the Bookmarks window.

> **Caution** Be careful when deleting folders. The folder and all its contents disappear when deleted. If you inadvertently delete a folder containing bookmarks you wanted to keep, don't forget that you can recover them by choosing Undo from the Edit menu.

The Conclusion

In this project you have been introduced to the World Wide Web through Netscape Navigator 4.0. You have acquired important skills for navigating the Web using Navigator's navigational buttons and tools. You have also learned to save your place and to organize your travels on the Web using bookmarks and bookmark folders.

This concludes Project 1. You can either exit Netscape Communicator now or go on to work the Review Exercises and Assignments.

Summary and Exercises

Summary

- The location of Web pages on the Internet is designated by the URL (Uniform Resource Locator), a standardized address composed of three parts: protocol, domain name, and file name (including directory path).
- You can jump to Web sites with Netscape using URLs and the location field.
- You can move back and forward between Web sites you have visited during the current session using the Back and Forward buttons.
- You can return to the Netscape startup location using the Home button.
- Netscape's history feature allows you to jump directly to Web sites you have visited during the current session. To do this, select the desired site from the Go menu.
- Most Web pages contain links to other Web pages. Text links appear in a different color and are sometimes underlined. When the cursor is over a text or picture link, the cursor icon becomes a hand.
- You can click a link on a Web page to jump to the Web page referenced by that link.
- Netscape offers standard Print Preview and Print options under the File menu.
- Bookmarks permanently record the addresses of Web sites.
- To create a bookmark for the currently displayed page, select Add Bookmark from the Bookmarks menu.
- Bookmarks you have created are listed in the Bookmarks menu and in the Bookmarks window.
- You can delete a bookmark by selecting the bookmark in the Bookmarks window and choosing Delete from the Bookmarks window Edit menu.
- You can create folders to organize your bookmarks using the Insert Folder option in the Bookmarks window Item menu.
- You can rearrange bookmarks and folders by dragging them in the Bookmarks window.
- You can delete bookmarks and folders by selecting them in the Bookmarks window and choosing Delete from the Bookmarks window Edit menu.

Key Terms and Operations

Key Terms	Operations
bookmark	arrange bookmarks
CD-ROM	create, delete, and edit bookmarks
domain name	create bookmarks folders
file name	go back, forward, and home
folder	jump to Web sites using links
history	jump to Web sites using URLs
home page	use the Go menu to revisit Web sites
link	use Print Preview and Print
MS-DOS	
picture link	
protocol	
text link	

50

Study Questions

Multiple Choice

1. The three parts of a URL (Uniform Resource Locator) are
   a. protocol, denominator, and file name.
   b. prototype, domain name, and file folder.
   c. protocol, domain name, and file name.
   d. prototype, denominator, and file folder.

2. Netscape Navigator belongs to a group of applications know as Web
   a. crawlers.
   b. skimmers.
   c. browsers.
   d. surfers.

3. You know the cursor is on a picture or text link if the cursor is displayed using a(n)
   a. arrow icon.
   b. I-beam icon.
   c. flashing icon.
   d. hand icon.

4. The character used to separate the components of URLs is typically a
   a. /
   b. :
   c. \
   d. None of the above.

5. Bookmarks differ from the history feature in that bookmarks
   a. must be created by the user.
   b. do not disappear at the end of each Netscape session.
   c. mark only those sites the user wishes to remember or revisit.
   d. All of the above.

6. When a folder in the bookmarks window is deleted, all bookmarks contained in that folder are
   a. moved up to the root level.
   b. deleted.
   c. saved in the bookmarks.ini file.
   d. None of the above.

7. A bookmark folder can be moved by _____ a new location.
   a. designating
   b. dragging it to
   c. selecting
   d. specifying

8. Before you can delete a bookmark, you must _____ it in the Bookmarks window.
   a. identify
   b. select
   c. double-click
   d. save

50

9. To create a folder in the Bookmarks window, choose
   a. Add Folder from the Edit menu.
   b. New Folder from the Item menu.
   c. New Folder from the Edit menu.
   d. Insert Folder from the Item menu.

10. Bookmarks can be moved into a new folder by _____ them.
    a. moving
    b. selecting
    c. dragging
    d. editing

Short Answer

1. The Netscape feature that keeps track of Web pages that you have already visited during the current session is called _____.

2. Web pages are actually just text documents that are created using a special language called _____.

3. Among the most powerful features of most Web pages are _____, which allow you to jump between Web sites.

4. _____ allow you to link graphics, sounds, and movies to Web pages.

5. Creating a _____ allows you to display related bookmarks in a submenu in the Bookmarks menu.

6. You can use _____ to group and organize bookmarks displayed in the Bookmarks menu.

7. Bookmarks and folders can be rearranged in the Bookmarks window by _____ them to a new location.

8. A bookmark can be deleted only from the Bookmarks _____.

9. Bookmarks contained in a folder in the Bookmarks window are displayed in a _____ in the Bookmarks window.

10. A bookmark may be deleted using Delete in the Bookmarks window Edit menu or by pressing _____.

For Discussion

1. How is the World Wide Web different from having multiple subject-specific CD ROMs? (CD-ROM stands for compact disk read only memory.)

2. Why is it important to know how to use the history feature of your Web browser? What are its limitations?

3. How is creating bookmarks different from the Go menu?

4. Why would you want to create folders to organize your bookmarks?

Review Exercises

1. Start Your Job Search
At the beginning of this project you were presented with a Challenge: use the Internet to help you in your job search after graduation. Now you can take the first steps in meeting that challenge.

1. Examine the Web links provided by Netscape's What's New? and What's Cool? options on the Guide menu. Look for links to corporations with which you are familiar.

2. At each interesting corporate home page you locate, try to find the company's employment opportunities page, and bookmark and print at least four such pages.

3. Place all of your new employment-related bookmarks in the Employment bookmarks folder.

4. Use the Save As option in the Bookmarks window File menu to save your bookmarks as a text file. Then open your bookmarks file using your favorite word processor, and print your bookmarks file.

2. Organize Your Job Search

Now that you know how to organize bookmarks into folders, you can organize all of your new employment-related bookmarks.

1. Go to the Career Magazine page located at http://careermag.com.

2. Locate and select a picture link called Career Links. A number of interesting career- and job-related Web pages are linked to the Career Magazine Career-Related Links page.

3. Visit Web sites that look interesting. Bookmark and print those to which you might wish to return later in your job search. Use Print Setup to ensure that the URL of each page prints in the header.

4. Place the new bookmarks you have created into the Employment bookmarks folder.

5. Repeat Step 4 from Review Exercise 1 above.

Assignments

1. More Information About the Internet

Go to the Web site located at http://info.isoc.org/guest/zakon/Internet, and check out some of the Internet History pages. Write and print a one-page summary of the growth of the Internet as described in these pages.

2. Folders Within Folders

Create two new bookmarks folders. Give these folders names that identify them as subcategories of Employment (for example, Corporations, Resume Banks, etc.). Place these new folders inside the Employment folder. Group your employment-related bookmarks into these new folders. Print your bookmarks using the method provided in Step 4 of Review Exercise 1 above.

Searching the Web with Netscape Navigator 4.0

To use the Internet effectively for researching any subject or for locating specific information, you must learn to use search engines and directories on the Web.

Objectives

After completing this project, you will be able to:

➤ **Understand the difference between search engines and directories**

➤ **Find search engines and directories on the Web**

➤ **Use search engines and directories**

➤ **Interpret search results**

➤ **Find specific text on a Web page**

The Challenge

You are finishing your undergraduate degree and preparing to enter the job market following graduation. In the previous project, you were inspired to learn how to get around on the World Wide Web (the Web) by the prospect of finding valuable employment information there. You now know how to surf the Web using Netscape Navigator 4.0, and you are ready to begin searching for employment information. But how do you *find* Web sites related to jobs or jobs in your specific field?

The Solution

You already know that the Web is a vast virtual landscape. There are Web pages out there on just about any topic. In fact, there are well over a million Web pages currently in existence with hundreds more appearing each day. So with all that information, how do you sift through it to find information on something specific?

To search the Web for employment information, you must learn something about some Web tools called *search engines* and *directories*. In this project you will become an expert at using these powerful tools to search for any information on the Web.

What Are Search Engines and Directories?

Search engines and *directories* are actually Web pages. These Web pages, however, have been designed for the express purpose of helping you find what you're looking for on the Web. Traditionally, the difference between a search engine and a directory has been its strategy for getting you to where you want to go; Search engines use a bottom-up strategy while directories use a top-down approach.

Search engines rely on you to provide the **search parameters**. Rather than beginning with the broadest possible description of the information you want, you begin with a specific word or phrase. In this sense, you are starting your search at the most detailed level, or at the bottom. Hence, the term **bottom-up search strategy**.

Directories, on the other hand, provide you with a number of **topics** from which to choose. The **top-down search strategy** of directories involves selecting a top-level category, like business, and working your way through subsequent menus of subtopics until you arrive at a list of Web sites matching your specific requirements. There is a great variety of directories available on the Web. Some directories are limited to a particular topic or field. Some cover the entire Internet.

Arts	Entertainment	Investing	Recreation	Society
Business	Government	Media	Reference	Sports
Computers	Health	Movies	Regional	Travel
Education	Internet	Music	Science	Weather

Like most things on the Web, the concepts of search engines and directories are in flux. Currently, most directories contain search engines, and many search engines have been augmented to include directories. Thus the traditional distinction between search engines and directories has become a bit fuzzy.

Using Search Engines

In Project 1 you visited a Web page maintained by Netscape called Netscape Net Search. With this Web page, Netscape makes it easy for you to access a host of good Web searching services. In this project you will visit the Netscape Net Search again. But this time you will dig in and do some exploring using the Internet search services linked to that page.

Before you can begin using Internet search services, you must first start Netscape Communicator. This procedure is covered in the Overview if you need a refresher.

TASK 1: TO ACCESS NET SEARCH

1   With Netscape Navigator 4.0 running, select 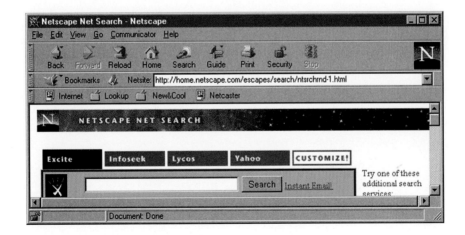 in the Navigation toolbar.

The Netscape Net Search page appears. Notice that a number of search services are listed on tabs. At the time of this writing, these services included Excite, Infoseek, Lycos, and Yahoo!.

2   Using the vertical scroll bar, scroll down to view the entire Net Search page.

Notice that a number of other search services are listed in addition to those featured on the tabs at the top of the page.

3   Scroll back to the top of the page.

4 If it's not already selected, select the Infoseek tab.

A new Netscape Net Search page is loaded. This page contains a search interface linked directly to the Infoseek Guide search service.

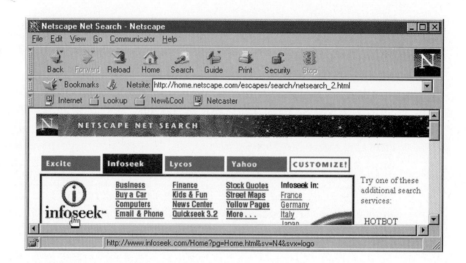

Jumping to the Infoseek Search Engine

You can perform a search directly from the Net Search page using any of the search services displayed on the tabs. Alternatively, you can jump directly to the home page of any of these search services using the links provided by Netscape.

TASK 2: TO GET TO INFOSEEK'S SEARCH ENGINE

1 Select the Infoseek logo on the currently displayed Net Search page

Notice that the Infoseek logo is a picture link. Netscape takes you to the Infoseek home page.

2 Scroll down to view the entire page.

Notice that, in addition to a search criteria field, Infoseek also offers a directory. Infoseek qualifies as both a search engine and a directory because it offers both a field for search parameters and a list of topics.

Using Infoseek's Search Engine

You won't be learning to use all of the search engines linked to the Netscape Net Search page in this project. You will instead focus on learning to use just one of the search services, Infoseek. Most search engines are functionally very similar, though, so once you've learned to use one, learning others will be a snap.

Infoseek has provided some basic search Tips on its home page. These tips will help the uninitiated become familiar with the syntax used by Infoseek for search parameters. Search Tips also offers a more detailed tutorial on how to perform different types of searches using the Infoseek search engine. A link to this document is provided on the Infoseek page.

TASK 3: USING SEARCH PARAMETERS IN INFOSEEK

1   Locate the <u>Tips</u> text link near the search criteria field on the Infoseek page.

2   Click the <u>Tips</u> text link.

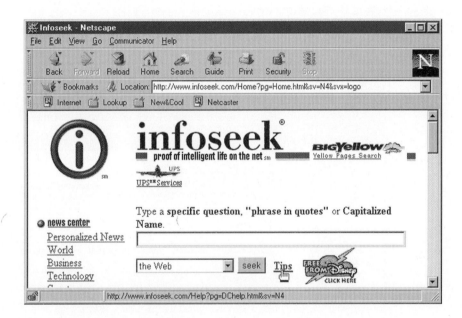

An Infoseek help page appears. Use the vertical scroll bar to find text links that may be helpful in searches using the Infoseek search engine.

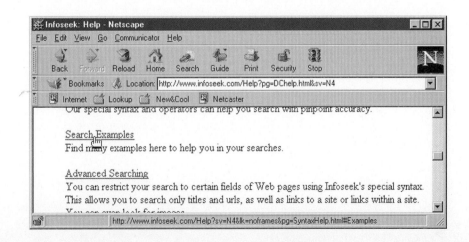

3 Select a link such as <u>Search Examples</u>, and read the contents of the page.

4 When you have finished going over the Infoseek search tips, use the Back button to return to the Netscape Net Search page displaying the Infoseek search interface.

You are now ready to enter search parameters in the Infoseek search field. Recall that your original purpose in exploring the Web was to search for job opportunities in your field.

TASK 4: TO SEARCH THE INTERNET USING INFOSEEK

1 Type employment in the Infoseek search field on the Net Search page.

2 Select the Seek button.

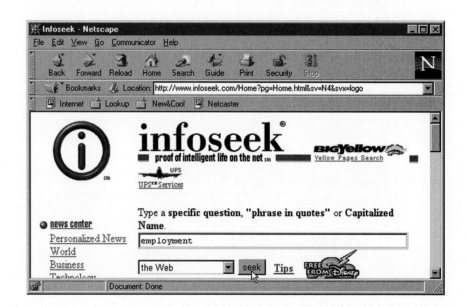

Infoseek searches for the word "employment" among Web pages currently indexed in its database. Generally, the header, description, and body of documents are searched, although different search engines perform searches differently. After a brief delay, Infoseek returns a search results page.

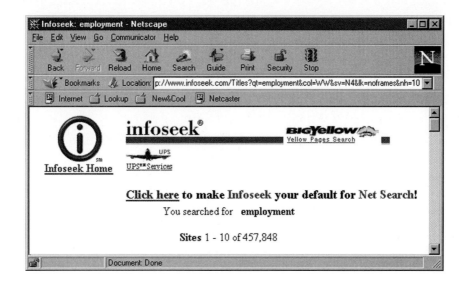

3   Scroll down a bit to begin to view the names and descriptions of documents matching your search parameter, employment.

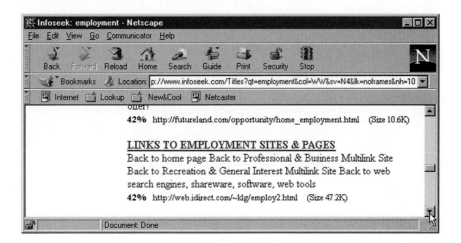

Searches often result in hundreds or even hundreds of thousands of "hits," that is, Internet documents matching your search parameters. Because "employment" is a fairly common word, your search probably resulted in a list of many thousands of documents (457,848 in the example above!), and your results page displays the first ten documents on that list.

Infoseek displays a text link near the top and bottom of search results pages that allows you to view the next ten documents (or previous ten) of those returned.

TASK 5: TO NAVIGATE THROUGH INFOSEEK SEARCH RESULTS

1   Locate and select the <u>next 10</u> text link on the Infoseek search results page.

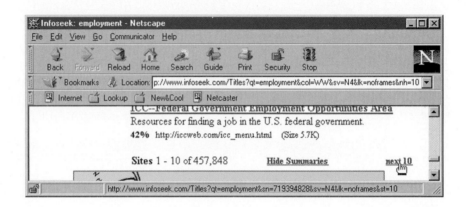

A new results page is loaded, displaying found documents 11–20.

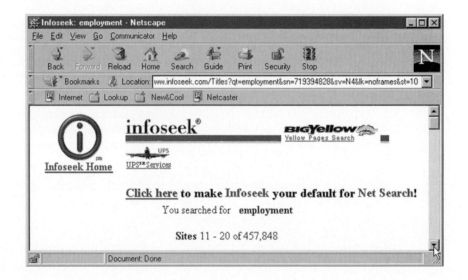

2   Scroll down a bit.

Notice that next to the <u>next 10</u> text link, a link called <u>prev 10</u> appears as well. You can use these two links to navigate forward and backward through search results. Most search engines offer similar links.

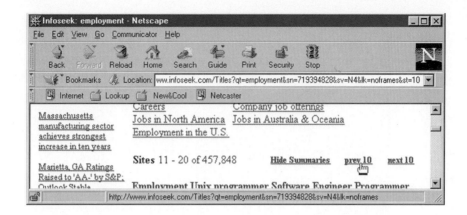

> **Tip** In some search services like Infoseek, you can also use the Back and Forward buttons to navigate through your search results. Some search services, however simply update the same page with incremental search results. In such cases you cannot use the Back and Forward buttons to navigate through search results.

3 Continue navigating through the search results list using the <u>prev 10</u> and <u>next 10</u> text links.

4 Visit any employment-related Web sites that interest you by clicking the titles.

5 When you have finished exploring, return to a Net Search page using the history feature.

Visiting Other Search Engines

There are other search engines available on the Net Search page, including Excite, Lycos, and Yahoo!. Netscape is continuously updating its Net Search page to include links to Internet search tools that it feels are particularly useful.

TASK 6: TO ACCESS OTHER SEARCH ENGINES

1 Scroll down the Netscape Net Search page until you come to a list of additional search services.

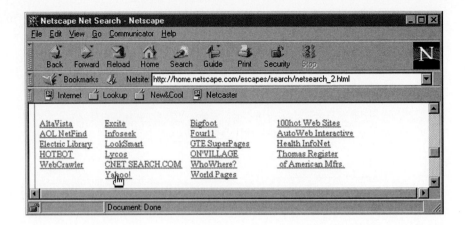

2   Click the <u>Yahoo!</u> text link.

Netscape takes you to the Yahoo! search service.

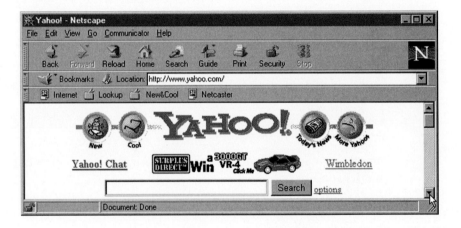

3   Scroll down to view the entire Yahoo! home page.

Notice the similarities between Yahoo! and Infoseek. Both provide a field for entering search parameters and also a list of topics from which to choose.

Remember   The Web is constantly changing. The Web pages you see on your screen will very likely look different than those shown in this module.

Using Directories

You have seen links to most of the popular search engines available on the Web. You have learned to use one search tool linked to the Net Search page, Infoseek, to perform key word searches. Now you will learn to use a Web directory tool that is also linked to the Netscape Net Search page.

TASK 7: TO GET TO EXCITE'S DIRECTORY

1 Go to the Netscape Net Search page.

2 Select the Excite tab on the Net Search page.

Netscape takes you to the Excite Net Search page.

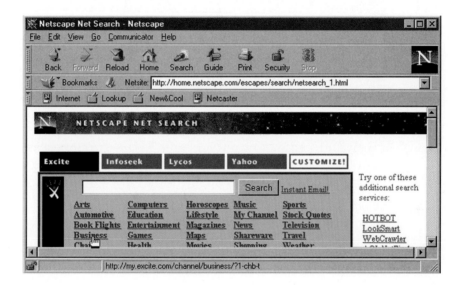

Like Infoseek, Excite qualifies as both a search engine and a directory because it offers both a field for search parameters and a list of topics.

Using the Excite Directory

As was the case with search engines, you won't be learning to use all of the directories linked to the Net Search page in this project. You will instead focus on learning to use just one of the directories, Excite. You will find that most other directories are functionally similar, and learning to use others will be easy.

TASK 8: TO BEGIN AN EXCITE DIRECTORY SEARCH

1 Select the Excite <u>Business</u> topic on the Excite Net Search page.

An Excite directory page listing the available topics under the Business topic is loaded and appears on the screen.

2 Use the vertical scroll bar to view Excite's Business Subtopics.

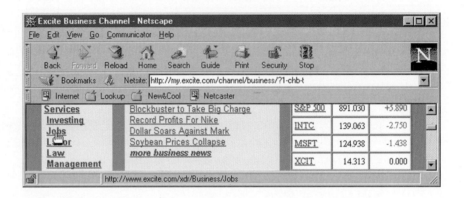

You are now ready to continue your Excite directory search by selecting a subtopic of Business. Recall that your original purpose in exploring the Web was to search for job opportunities in your field.

3 Select <u>Jobs</u> from Business Subtopics listed.

Excite displays a <u>Jobs</u> subtopics page.

4 Scroll down to view all of the Jobs Subtopics listed.

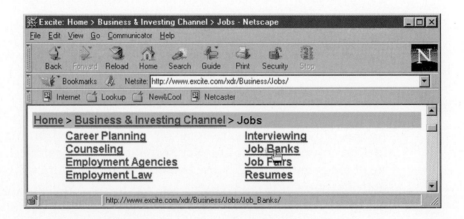

5 Select <u>Job Banks</u> from Jobs Subtopics listed.

Excite displays a list of reviewed Job Bank Web sites. From this list you can select links to any one of the Web sites listed.

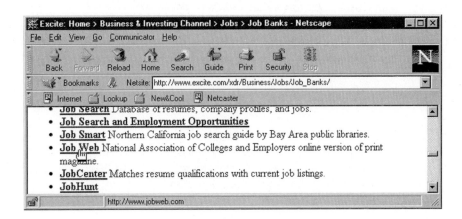

TASK 9: TO NAVIGATE THROUGH EXCITE DIRECTORY SEARCH RESULTS

1   Scroll down to view all of the Web site reviews. Use the descriptions provided for each site to help you decide if it is worth a visit.

2   If it is displayed as shown above, select Job Web from the Excite list of reviewed Job Bank sites. If Job Web is not in the list, select another site that sounds like it might be helpful in your job search.

If you were able to select the link to Job Web, Netscape delivers you to the Job Web home page.

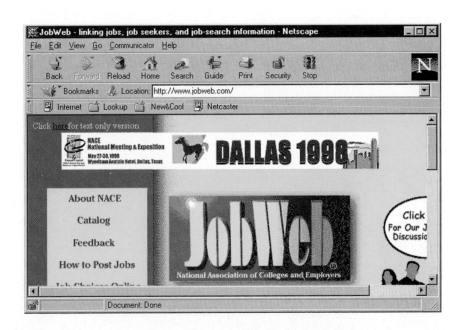

3 Explore the Job Web site by clicking on links displayed on its home page.

> **Remember** Remember to use the Back and Forward buttons and the history feature to help you explore the Job Web site, to explore other employment sites listed in your search results, and to explore other topics within the Excite Jobs category.

4 When you have finished exploring the Job Web site, or any other jobs-related sites you have visited using the Excite directory, use the history feature to return to the Netscape Net Search page.

Visiting Other Directories

As already discussed, most search services offer both search engines and directories, and you can access a number of popular search services from the Net Search page.

TASK 10: TO ACCESS OTHER DIRECTORIES

1 Scroll down the Netscape Net Search page until you come to a list of additional search services.

2 Select the link to a search service you have not yet visited.

Does this search service offer a directory? Try using this directory to search for employment-related Web sites.

Searching for Text on a Web Page

In addition to searching for Internet documents on specific topics, you will frequently need to search for specific text in a document you are viewing. As you know, Web pages can be very long documents, the equivalent of many printed pages. What if you want to find a particular word or phrase within such a document? The Find function is available for just that purpose—finding text on a Web page.

TASK 11: TO USE THE FIND FUNCTION

1 Go to the Wall Street Journal Interactive Edition Web page at: **wsj.com**

2   Click the page display area to select the displayed frame.

3   Choose Find in Frame from the Edit menu.

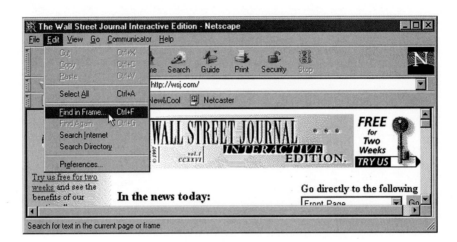

The Find dialog box is displayed. Notice that this dialog box allows you to determine whether Navigator will find only text that matches the case (uppercase and lowercase letters) of the text you enter. It also allows you to determine the direction in which Netscape will search the document: going down from the top or going up from the bottom.

4   Type **jobs** in the Find what field, and select   Find Next

Netscape locates and selects the first occurrence of the text you entered. In this example, an instance of the word "jobs" was located.

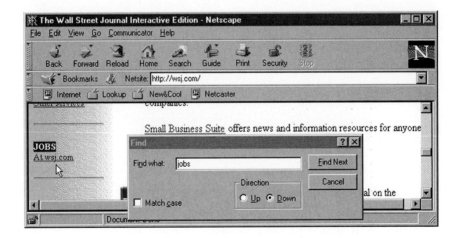

Tip   You may need to move the Find dialog out of the way to see the found text. Do this by using the mouse to drag the Find dialog box by its title bar.

5   Select 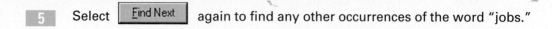 again to find any other occurrences of the word "jobs."

> **Tip**   You can still use the Find Next function even if the Find dialog is not displayed. Simply press F3, and Netscape will again search for the text last entered in the Find dialog.

When Netscape has located all occurrences of the given text, it displays the Search String Not Found dialog box.

6   Select   OK   in the Search String Not Found dialog box.

7   Select   Cancel   on the Find dialog box to exit the Find function.

The Conclusion

In this project you have learned to search for specific information on the Web using two different types of tools—search engines and directories. You've also learned how to search for specific text on a Web page using the Find funtion. Now it's time to get your feet wet communicating using the Internet. In the next project you will learn to use Netscape to send and even receive electronic mail (e-mail).

This section concludes Project 2. You can either exit Netscape Communicator or go on to work the Study Questions, Review Exercises, and Assignments.

Summary and Exercises

Summary

- Search engines and directories are special Web pages designed to help you find information on the Web.
- Directories use a top-down search strategy, starting with topics.
- Search engines use a bottom-up strategy starting with key word(s).
- Many popular search engines are linked to Netscape's Net Search page.
- Most search engines are functionally similar and easy to use.
- Infoseek is one of the search services linked to the Net Search page.
- Infoseek contains both a search engine and a directory.
- Search engines produce the best results when you learn to use the search parameter syntax and pose specific queries.
- Many popular directories are linked to Netscape's Net Search page.
- Excite is one of the search services linked to the Net Search page.
- Like Infoseek, Excite provides both a directory and a search engine.
- Most directories are functionally similar, providing nested lists of topics from which to choose.
- You can find text within a Web page using the Find function.

Key Terms and Operations

Key Terms
bottom-up search strategy
directory
search engine
search parameter
top-down search strategy
topic

Operations
search by key word(s)
search by topic
navigate through search results
find text

Study Questions

Multiple Choice

1. Search engines and directories are
   a. used to help locate specific information on the Web.
   b. Web pages.
   c. sometimes both included in Internet search tools.
   d. All of the above.

2. Search engines work best when
   a. very general, common words are used for search parameters.
   b. search parameters are posed in plural form.
   c. you wish to perform a search based on a key word or phrase.
   d. All of the above.

3. Infoseek Guide has its own _____ that helps users improve the quality of search results.
   a. search parameter syntax
   b. autosearch strategy language
   c. query domain language
   d. context-sensitive query form

4. The Find function in Netscape allows you to locate
   a. Web pages on specific topics.
   b. all of the Web pages you have viewed during the current session.
   c. specific words or phrases within a Web document.
   d. None of the above.

5. _____ is a popular search service available on the Web.
   a. WebSpan
   b. CyberScape
   c. Yahoo!
   d. Columbus

6. Directories are used to perform _____ searches.
   a. categorical
   b. key word
   c. name
   d. phrase

7. You can use the _____ and _____ buttons to navigate through many search results.
   a. Back, Home
   b. Forward, Back
   c. Delete, Home
   d. None of the above.

8. When searching the Web, remember that _____ documents are often linked together.
   a. unrelated
   b. similar
   c. incompatible
   d. special

9. When search parameters are carefully composed,
   a. search results will include only documents of interest.
   b. all irrelevant information will be eliminated from search results.
   c. search results may still include unwanted information.
   d. None of the above.

10. Different search engines may search the
   a. document header.
   b. entire text of the document.
   c. document's text links.
   d. All of the above.

Short Answer

1. A _____ uses key words provided by the user to perform its searches.

2. Search services allow you to find _____ information on the Internet.

3. While search services are used to locate specific _____ the _____ function is used to locate text on a Web page.

4. Different search services often use _____ search strategies and generate _____ results.

5. You may locate specific text on a Web page using the _____ function.

6. _____ are designed to perform categorical searches.

7. Search results pages generally provide _____ to the documents listed.

8. _____ was a pioneer of Internet search services and is still among the premier search services available on the Web.

9. When performing searches on the Web, it is often helpful to use _____ to avoid losing documents of interest.

10. Some search services provide a brief _____ of each document in the search results list.

For Discussion

1. Describe some situations when it makes more sense to use a directory to perform an Internet search. When is it better to use a search engine?

2. How do you think search services work? Why do different search tools often produce different results based on the same search parameters?

3. Search services such as Infoseek Guide, Yahoo!, and Excite are business ventures. Where do you think their revenues come from?

4. How might Web site owners help their Web pages be among the first documents listed in search results? (Web site developers use a number of tricks to accomplish this!)

Review Exercises _____

1. Mark Your Place

At the beginning of this project you were presented with a Challenge: use the Internet to help you in your job search after graduation. Now you can take the first steps in meeting that challenge.

1. Using a search engine or directory of your choice, find the Job Web site again, and print the page.

2. Place a bookmark on the Job Web home page.

3. Move the new bookmark into an appropriate folder using the Bookmarks window.

4. Use the Save As option in the Bookmarks window File menu to save your bookmarks to a file. Open the bookmarks file using your favorite word processing application, and print the file.

2. Continue Your Job Search

In this project, we said that most search engines and directories are functionally similar. Use the skills you've acquired in this project to locate and use the search service Yahoo!.

1. Use Yahoo! to locate five more employment-related Web sites you feel will be useful in your job search. Print each page using Print Setup to ensure that the URL for each is printed in the header.

2. Bookmark each site.

3. Place those bookmarks in appropriate folders using the Bookmarks window.

4. Print your bookmarks by repeating Step 4 from Review Exercise 1.

Assignments

1. Using Other Search Services
Try performing searches for employment-related Web sites using other search services linked to the Net Search page. Print the first page of results for your search in two other search services. Use both search engines and directories. Bookmark sites you feel may be useful in your job search. Organize those bookmarks using folders and separators. Print your Bookmarks window.

2. Exploring Search.com
Go to www.search.com. What kind of a Web page is this? Is it a search service like Infoseek, or is it more like Netscape's Net Search page? Why do you suppose Search.com is rapidly becoming a very popular point at which to begin an Internet search? Answer these questions using a word processor, and print your answers. Try accessing Excite, Alta Vista, Yahoo!, and Infoseek from this Web site.

3. Using Search Services to Find Search Services
In this project you visited the search services linked to Netscape's Net Search and Net Directory pages. There are other search services emerging all the time. How do you suppose you find them? You guessed it! Use the search engine of your choice to look for other search engines and information about search engines. Use a word processesor to make and print a list of search services you find using search engines and directories.

Using Netscape Messenger for E-mail

One of the most powerful resources provided by the Internet is electronic mail or e-mail. In this project, you will learn to use Messenger, the e-mail component of Netscape Communicator, to communicate using e-mail.

Objectives

After completing this project, you will be able to:

➤ **Understand basic electronic mail concepts and terms**

➤ **Configure Netscape Messenger for e-mail**

➤ **Compose an e-mail message**

➤ **View, send, receive, and print e-mail messages**

➤ **Delete e-mail messages**

The Challenge

You are nearing graduation and are preparing to enter the job market. In the previous projects you found that the Web offers a tremendous number of resources for finding a good job. In fact, you have now located and bookmarked a number of employment-related Web sites and have found some companies you would like to contact.

Now you must consider your options for communicating with these companies. You have heard a lot about e-mail and wonder if that would be an option for requesting an application packet from some of the human resource departments you want to contact. You know you have an e-mail address (although you may not know what it is), since you have a computer account at your school. But how do you go about sending e-mail? Can you use Netscape Communicator to do it?

The Solution

Messenger, the e-mail component of Netscape Communicator, offers a full-featured e-mail interface that rivals some of the best (and easiest to use) e-mail applications around. So the next step is to learn how to use Netscape Messenger to compose, send, receive, and manage e-mail for your job search.

What Is E-mail?

Electronic mail, or e-mail, is one of the most popular and heavily used services provided by the Internet. E-mail is simply the word we use for sending messages from one computer to another. E-mail can be set up as a local service within an office, or it can be set up with access to the Internet. With an e-mail address and access to the Internet, you can send messages anywhere in the world. One of the greatest advantages of e-mail is that in most cases messages arrive at their destination just moments after they are sent. E-mail is one of the most powerful reasons that mail transported by the U.S. Postal Service has popularly become known as "snail mail." The speed and economy of e-mail is hard to beat.

Understanding E-mail Addresses

Every e-mail address must follow a standard format: It is composed of two parts, a *user name* and a domain name, separated by an @ sign.

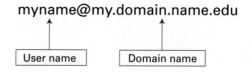

Remember the discussion of domain names back in Project 1? Well, here it is again: The domain name identifies the computer system that handles your e-mail. This is the computer that will recognize your user name. Your **user name** identifies you and is unique within the computer system. Remember that domain names are used to identify every computer on the Internet. Each part of the domain name is separated by a dot (.) and tells you something about the location of the computer. In the example shown on the previous page, *edu* indicates that the computer is part of an educational institution (as opposed to com or org, which are used to designate other types of organizations); *name* represents the name of the organization; and *my.domain* indicates the name of the computer at that organization where your e-mail service is located. The domain name may be as short as asu.edu or aol.com. It can also be long and complex, as in ensmtp1.eas.asu.edu or sba1102.sba.pdx.edu.

Parts of an E-mail Address

E-mail messages typically have three parts: a *header,* a *body,* and a *signature.* Your e-mail messages will look somewhat different depending on the e-mail software you use. We will focus here on how Netscape Messenger displays e-mail.

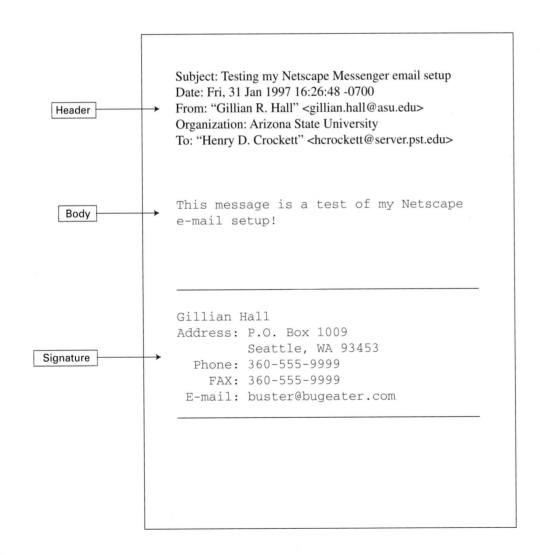

Header →

Subject: Testing my Netscape Messenger email setup
Date: Fri, 31 Jan 1997 16:26:48 -0700
From: "Gillian R. Hall" <gillian.hall@asu.edu>
Organization: Arizona State University
To: "Henry D. Crockett" <hcrockett@server.pst.edu>

Body →

This message is a test of my Netscape
e-mail setup!

Signature →

Gillian Hall
Address: P.O. Box 1009
         Seattle, WA 93453
  Phone: 360-555-9999
    FAX: 360-555-9999
 E-mail: buster@bugeater.com

The *header* displays the subject and date of the e-mail message. It also displays information (including the e-mail address) about both the sender and recipient of the message. The *body* of the e-mail message is where the actual message is displayed. In the example shown on the previous page, the message is quite short; however, e-mail messages can be as long as you like. Finally, the *signature* is an optional part of the message that you can configure Messenger to place at the end of every e-mail message you send. The signature contains information about you, like your name, address, and phone number. Some people include a favorite quote or even a link to their personal Web page.

Different E-mail Applications

There are a number of applications available for using e-mail. All of these provide an interface for sending, receiving, storing, and deleting e-mail messages. Some even provide features for organizing, sorting, replying to, and forwarding e-mail messages. Most provide some sort of address book in which you can store frequently used e-mail addresses, and many allow you to address a message to more than one person. Because there are so many similarities between e-mail applications, once you have learned to use one such application, learning others will be surprisingly easy.

While Netscape Messenger provides a nicely complete list of e-mail features, many people prefer to use other applications such as Eudora, Pegasus, Microsoft Mail, or Pine for accessing e-mail services. In this project, you will be using Netscape Messenger for e-mail, but it is important to be aware that there are other popular e-mail applications available. In fact, it is likely that your school provides an e-mail application other than Netscape Messenger.

If you are interested in learning to use another e-mail application, try searching for it by name using a search engine or directory. For example, a complete tutorial on using the Eudora e-mail package is located at the following address: http://www.netspot.unisa.edu.au/eudora/contents.html. You can even download a copy of the Eudora e-mail application from the Internet!

There is a tremendous amount of information and support available on the Internet for users of all e-mail applications. If your school uses something other than Netscape Messenger, you can be a rebel and use Netscape anyway, or you can learn more about the application preferred by your school by locating information about that application on the Web.

Launching Netscape Messenger

Remember that all the components of Communicator are tightly integrated, so you can easily jump from one to another almost without noticing! Therefore, there are a number of ways to launch Netscape Messenger: You can first launch Netscape Navigator 4.0 as covered in the Overview of this module, and then choose Messenger Mailbox from the Communicator menu.

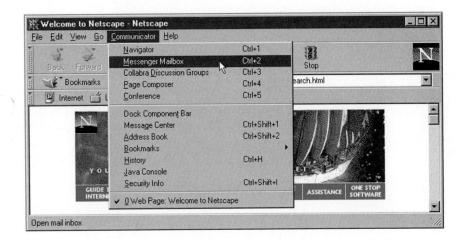

Or you can choose the Mailbox icon from the Communicator component bar.

Alternatively, depending upon the way in which Netscape Communicator is installed at your school, you may be able to launch Netscape Messenger directly from the Windows95 start menu.

TASK 1: TO LAUNCH NETSCAPE MESSENGER

1   Click the Start button **Start** and point to Programs.

2   Point to the Netscape Communicator folder and then to Netscape Messenger in the pull-down menus.

The Netscape Messenger program is launched.

Just as when you launch Navigator, the Netscape Communicator startup screen appears and remains on your screen while your computer establishes its connection to the network.

The startup screen disappears when a network connection has been confirmed. It is replaced by a Netscape Messenger message list window and the Netscape Communicator component bar.

Exploring the Message List Window

The message list window displayed by Netscape Messenger is organized much like the Navigator 4.0 window. The message list window includes a title bar, menu bar, toolbar, and scroll bars when displaying images too large to be fully displayed. These are features you will find in nearly all Windows applications. The message list windows also includes a number of other features important to managing your e-mail including message folders, a *message header display area*, and a *message display area* (displayed by clicking the message display button).

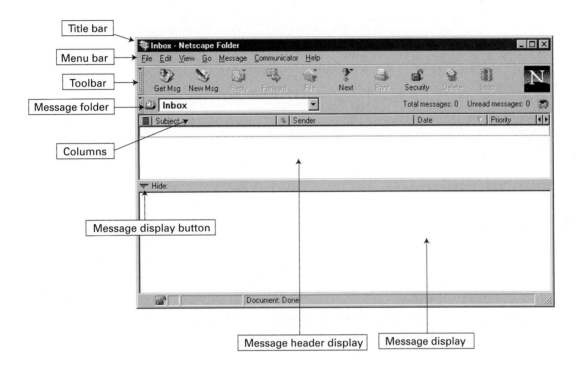

Managing Columns

The message header display area of the Messenger message list window is divided into ***columns***. These columns provide the sender name, subject, date, flagged status, read status, length, and other properties of each e-mail message contained in the message folder named in the message folder field. By resizing, rearranging, adding, and deleting these columns, you can customize the look for the message list window to suit your needs.

TASK 2: TO RESIZE MESSAGE HEADER COLUMNS

1   Point to the divider between two column headers.

The mouse pointer becomes a double-ended arrow (⊣⊢).

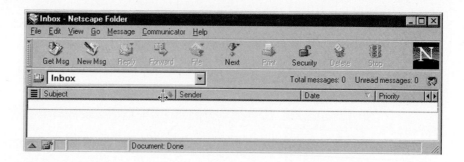

2   Drag the divider to the left or right.

Notice how the column to the left of the mouse pointer is resized as you drag the column divider.

TASK 3: TO REARRANGE MESSAGE HEADER COLUMNS

1   Point to a column, and drag it to the left or right.

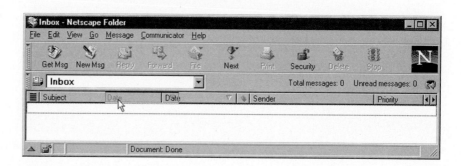

2   Drop the column header when it appears to have been repositioned as desired.

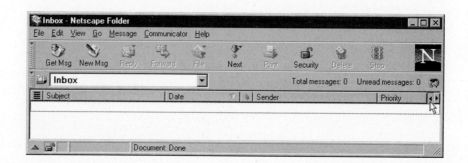

TASK 4: TO ADD OR REMOVE MESSAGE HEADER COLUMNS

1 Click the left-facing arrow button on the far right side of the row of message header columns.

Notice that a new column is added.

2 Continue clicking the left-facing arrow button until all column headers are displayed.

Notice that in addition to sender, subject, flag, and date columns, Messenger also offers a number of additional message header columns.

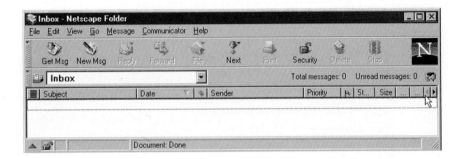

3 To remove columns, simply click the right-facing arrow button on the column header bar.

Notice that you can remove as many columns as you like. This feature combined with the ability to resize and rearrange columns allows you complete freedom in customizing the way message headers are displayed.

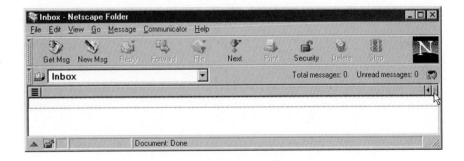

4 Using the left-facing arrow button, restore the columns originally displayed (sender, subject, date, etc.).

Managing the Message Display Area

The message display area is where Messenger displays the actual content of the currently selected e-mail message. Depending upon the preferences saved for the copy of Communicator you are using, the message display area may or may not already be open.

TASK 5: TO OPEN AND CLOSE THE MESSAGE DISPLAY AREA

1 Click the message display button in the lower left corner of the message list window.

Notice that the message display area appears and the message display button changes to a down-facing arrow.

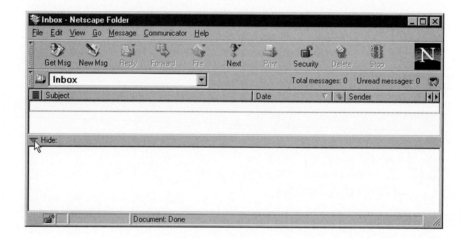

2 To hide the message display area, simply click the message display button again.

> **Tip** You may want to increase the size of the message list window when the message display area is showing.

TASK 6: TO SIZE THE MESSAGE DISPLAY AREA

1 Point to the divider between the message header and message display area.

Notice that the mouse pointer changes to a double-ended arrow.

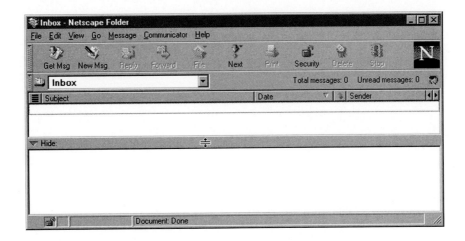

2 Drag the divider up and down to adjust the size of the message header and message display areas.

Remember that you can also adjust the size of the message list window itself to increase or decrease the size of the message display area.

Configuring Messenger for E-mail

To use Netscape Messenger for e-mail, you must first configure it properly. You will need some information about your e-mail services, like your e-mail address and the address(es) of the computer(s) that provide your e-mail services. Most schools provide computer account services for their students, so we are assuming here that you have a computer account at your school. Your instructor will be able to help you with this and with the other information you will need to configure Messenger for e-mail. To complete this project, you must have a computer account at your school with a user name, *password* (your personal and confidential access code), and e-mail address.

TASK 7: TO ACCESS E-MAIL PREFERENCES

1 Choose Preferences from the Edit menu in the Messenger message list window.

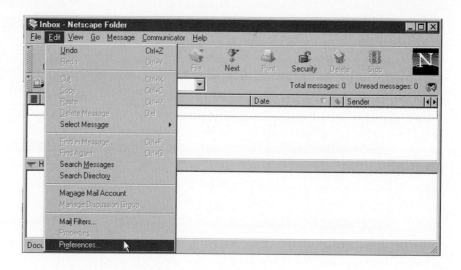

The Preferences dialog box is displayed. You will use this dialog box to configure Messenger for your e-mail.

Notice the tree menu of preferences categories on the left side of the Preferences window. Subcategories of Mail & Groups include Identity, Messages, Mail Server, Groups Server, and Directory. The information required for using Messenger for e-mail is requested under the Identity and Mail Server categories. You can explore the rest of the preferences tabs on your own using Netscape Communicator Online Help to understand all the Mail & Groups Preferences options.

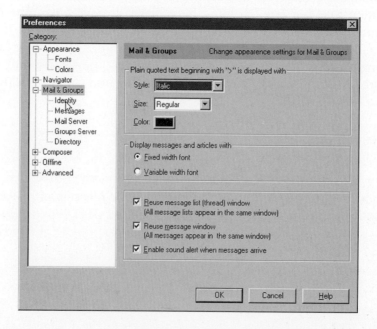

Configuring the Header for Your Outgoing E-mail Messages

Remember the header portion of e-mail messages discussed at the beginning of this project? Messenger's Mail and Groups Preferences allows you to specify information about yourself like your name and e-mail address that will be used in the header of messages you send.

TASK 8: TO CONFIGURE THE HEADER OF E-MAIL YOU SEND

1   Select the Identity category in the Preferences tree menu.

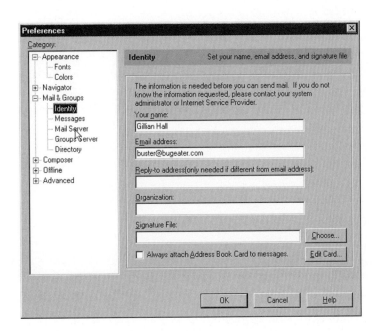

2   In the field labeled Your name, enter your name as you want it to appear in the header of your outgoing e-mail messages.

3   In the field labeled E-mail address, enter your e-mail address.

This is the e-mail address which will appear in the header of your outgoing messages. Ask your instructor for assistance if you don't know your e-mail address. As already discussed, we are assuming your school has provided you with a computer account including e-mail services.

Specifying Your E-mail Servers

You will now provide Messenger with the information it needs to deliver and receive your e-mail. This information includes your e-mail servers (the computers at your school that handle your e-mail services), your user name, and your computer account password.

TASK 9: TO SPECIFY YOUR E-MAIL SERVER(S)

1 Select the Mail Server category in the Preferences tree menu.

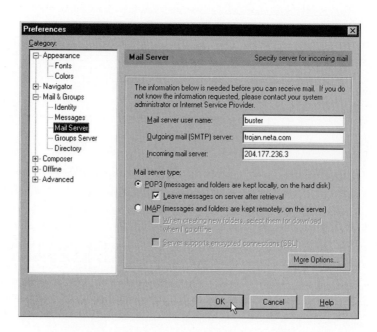

2 In the field labeled Mail server user name, enter the user name you have been assigned by your school.

As discussed at the beginning of this project, your user name is generally the first part of your e-mail address. For example, if your e-mail address is gillian.hall@asu.edu, your mail server user name is probably gillian.hall.

3 In the field labeled Outgoing mail (SMTP) server, enter the domain name or IP address of your outgoing mail or *SMTP (Simple Mail Transport Protocol)* server.

This is the computer that handles your outgoing mail. Your instructor will help you with this information if needed.

4 In the field labeled Incoming mail server, enter the domain name or IP address of your incoming mail or *POP (Post Office Protocol) server*.

This is the computer that handles your incoming mail. It is often the same as your SMTP server, but check with your instructor to be sure.

Alert! The information shown in the example screens provided is only an example. You must enter your own server addresses, user name, and so on. The ones shown here won't do you any good at all!

5   Select   OK   in the Preferences dialog.

Sending and Receiving E-mail Messages

Now comes the fun part. You are ready to compose and send your first e-mail message using Netscape Messenger. Start by sending a message to yourself.

TASK 10: TO COMPOSE AN E-MAIL MESSAGE

1   Select 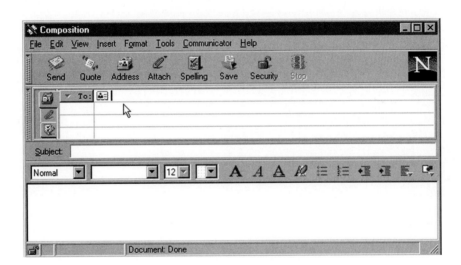 in the message list toolbar.

A message composition window is displayed. You will use this window to address and compose your first e-mail message.

2   In the field labeled To:, enter your e-mail address.

This is the field into which you will always enter the e-mail address of the message recipient.

3   In the field labeled Subject, type **My first message**

The subject of your message should briefly alert the message recipient to the subject matter of the body of the message.

4   In the message composition area at the bottom of the window, type **This is the body of my first e-mail message using Netscape Messenger, the cool e-mail component of Netscape Communicator.**

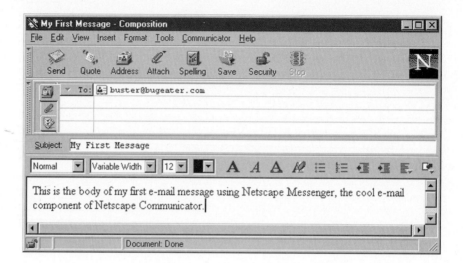

TASK 11: TO SEND AN E-MAIL MESSAGE

1 When you have finished composing your message, select [Send] on the message composition window toolbar.

Netscape Messenger contacts your e-mail server and sends the message. The message composition window disappears after the message has been successfully sent.

TASK 12: TO RECEIVE AN E-MAIL MESSAGE

1 A minute or two after sending your first e-mail message, select [Get Msg] on the message list window toolbar.

Messenger will attempt to log onto your e-mail server using your user name. It will then ask for your password. Depending on the way Netscape Communicator is set up at your school, you may be asked to enter your e-mail password each time you attempt to retrieve your mail using Messenger.

2 If Messenger requests your password, enter it in the dialog provided, and select [OK]

If you don't know your e-mail account password, you instructor will help you find out what it is.

> **Tip** Your e-mail password is very important and very confidential. It allows you and only you to view your e-mail. Anyone can find out your server information and your user name, but only you and your system administrator know your password, so don't tell anyone what it is!

If all goes well, Netscape Messenger will successfully log onto your e-mail server, check for any new messages, and download them.

If you have new messages, the headers of those messages will be displayed in the message header area. If you do not have new messages, Messenger will display the following dialog box.

Don't Panic If there is something wrong with your Mail Server configuration, you will get an error message regarding Messenger's ability to communicate with your server(s). If this happens, go back to the Mail Server screen in the Mail & News Preferences dialog box. Have your instructor help you track down the problem. It's probably just a typo, so don't worry.

3 To display the body of new e-mail messages you have received, select the message in the message header area.

Notice that Messenger displays e-mail just like Web pages. In fact, Messenger creates HTML documents of each e-mail message you receive to display it using the font and color preferences you specified in the Overview of this module.

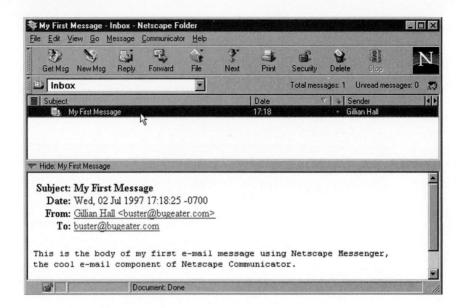

The body of the selected message is displayed in the message display area. (If necessary, open the message display area using the message display button.)

4   Use the scroll bars to view the entire body of the displayed message.

Printing E-mail Messages

Once you have downloaded and viewed a new e-mail message, you may wish to print the message. Printing e-mail messages is accomplished in much the same way as printing Web pages using Navigator 4.0. As is the case in Navigator 4.0, Messenger offers Print Preview, Print Setup, and Print Page options to help you get the best results possible.

TASK 13: TO PRINT AN E-MAIL MESSAGE

1   Select the desired message in the message header area of the message list window.

2   Choose Print from the File menu.

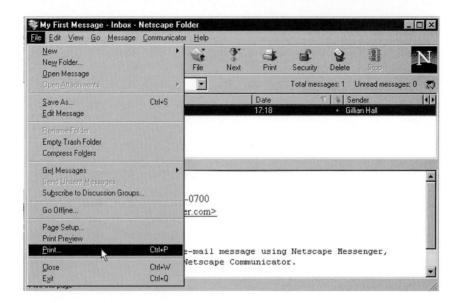

The Print window appears. The Print window allows you to specify which pages you wish to print, the print quality, the number of copies, and whether or not you wish to have multiple copies collated.

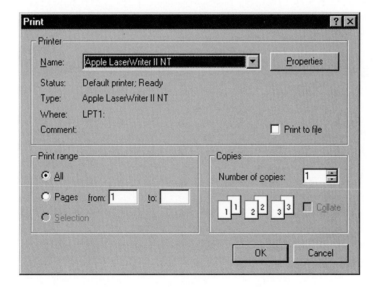

3 Make any changes you wish to the print options displayed.

4 Select OK

The selected e-mail message is printed on your computer's default printer.

Deleting E-mail Messages

After you have read an e-mail message, you may wish to delete it. Netscape puts deleted messages into a special ***Trash folder***. Messages are not actually deleted until you "empty the trash." This feature allows you to change your mind about deleting a message before it is really gone!

TASK 14: TO DELETE AN E-MAIL MESSAGE

1 Select the header of the message you sent to yourself in the header display area of the message list window.

2 Select [Delete] on the message list window toolbar.

> **Tip** You can also delete a message by selecting its header, and then selecting Delete Message from the Edit menu in the message list window.

The message header and body disappear from the message list window. The message is actually just moved to the Trash folder where it will stay until you "empty the trash."

TASK 15: TO EMPTY THE TRASH FOLDER

1 Select Empty Trash Folder from the File menu in the message list window.

2 The contents of the Trash folder are permanently deleted from your Messenger inbox.

The Conclusion

In this project you have learned the basics of setting up Netscape Messenger for e-mail and of using Messenger to send and receive e-mail messages. As we pointed out earlier in this project, Messenger is a complete and robust tool for communicating via e-mail. It offers a tremendous number of features not covered here. Use Netscape Communicator Online Help to learn more about taking full advantage of the e-mail features offered by Netscape Messenger.

This concludes Project 3. You can either exit Netscape Communicator or go on to work the Study Questions, Review Exercises, and Assignments.

Summary and Exercises

Summary

- Electronic mail (e-mail) is a special way of sending electronic messages from one computer to another.
- An e-mail address is a specially formatted address containing the recipient's user name and domain name of the e-mail service provider.
- E-mail messages generally contain three parts: the header, the body, and the signature.
- Netscape Messenger is the e-mail component of Communicator.
- Messenger must be specially configured for your e-mail before you can receive mail using this tool.
- Use the Mail Server tab on the Mail and Groups Preferences dialog to enter your e-mail server information.
- Use the Identity tab on the Mail and Groups Preferences dialog to enter your name and e-mail address for use in the header of e-mail messages you send.
- You can access your e-mail using the Messenger message list window.
- The message list window displays mail folders and message header columns for displaying e-mail messages.
- Message header columns can be rearranged, sized, removed, and deleted.
- The message display area is opened by selecting the message display button in the lower left of the message list window.
- View the body of a e-mail message by opening the message display area and selecting the desired message in the message header display area.
- To print an e-mail message, select it in the header display area of the message list window, and choose Print Page from the File menu.
- To delete an e-mail message, select it in the header display area of the message list window, and choose the Delete button from the toolbar.

Key Terms and Operations

Key Terms	Operations
body	specify Mail Server Preferences
column	configure Identity Preferences
header	open the message list window
message display area	rearrange and resize columns
message header area	add and remove columns
password	get your new e-mail messages
POP server	view e-mail messages
signature	print e-mail messages
SMTP server	delete e-mail messages
Trash folder	
user name	

94

Study Questions

Multiple Choice

1. Most e-mail messages are composed of the following three parts:
   a. identity, body, closing.
   b. introduction, text, name.
   c. header, body, signature.
   d. address, body, signature.

2. All e-mail addresses conform to a standard format containing a
   a. user name and address.
   b. identity and location.
   c. identity and domain name.
   d. user name and domain name.

3. The two parts of an e-mail address are separated by a(n) _____.
   a. .
   b. @
   c. &
   d. #

4. The signature portion of an e-mail message generally contains information about the
   a. subject of the e-mail message.
   b. date and time the message was sent.
   c. person who sent the message.
   d. All of the above.

5. The header portion of an e-mail message generally contains information about the
   a. subject of the e-mail message.
   b. date and time the message was sent.
   c. person who sent the message.
   d. All of the above.

6. Before Messenger can be used for your e-mail, you must configure the _____ screen of the Mail and Groups Preferences dialog box.
   a. Composition
   b. Organization
   c. Mail Server
   d. Identity

7. A _____ server generally handles your outgoing mail, while the _____ server generally handles your incoming mail.
   a. POP, Mail
   b. Mail, SMTP
   c. POP, SMTP
   d. SMTP, POP

8. To access your e-mail, you must provide Netscape with your user name, server information, and
   a. password.
   b. domain name.
   c. protocol.
   d. home page.

9. _____ is the name of another popular e-mail application.
   a. Eunice
   b. Eudora
   c. Eugene
   d. Unicorn

10. When you select the Delete button, the selected message is
   a. permanently deleted from your Inbox file.
   b. moved into the Trash folder.
   c. placed in the recycle bin.
   d. None of the above.

Short Answer

1. The _____ part of your e-mail address identifies the computer that handles your e-mail.

2. Your _____ should not be shared with anyone.

3. The _____ portion of an e-mail message is where the body of the message is displayed.

4. You can customize the way message headers are displayed by sizing, rearranging, adding, and deleting message header _____.

5. E-mail messages are displayed by Netscape Messenger as _____ documents, just like Web pages.

6. E-mail messages are composed using the _____ window.

7. When e-mail messages are deleted, they are actually just moved into the _____.

8. To permanently delete an e-mail message, you must "_____ the _____."

9. E-mail messages are printed by selecting the desired message header, and then choosing _____ from the _____ menu.

10. The message list window displays the contents of the _____ named in the message folder field.

For Discussion

1. Both Web page URLs and e-mail addresses contain domain names. Does domain name mean the same thing for both e-mail and Web page addresses?

2. You went to quite a bit of trouble in this project to set up your e-mail preferences using the Mail and Groups Preferences dialog box. If you are working with a networked version of Netscape Communicator, none of your preferences were saved when you exited. If you are using a computer to which others have access, perhaps you don't want any of your preferences saved (especially your e-mail configuration). Would it be helpful to be able to carry your own Netscape Communicator preferences file around with you on a floppy disk? How might this be useful?

Review Exercises

1. Sending More E-mail

So far, you have had very limited experience sending e-mail messages. In this exercise you will get some more practice!

1. Ask five of your classmates to exchange e-mail addresses. Ask each classmate with whom you exchange e-mail addresses to send you a message.

2. Address a message to each of these classmates. Enter your own e-mail address in the second To field in order to receive a copy of each message in your own Inbox.

3. Get new messages, and print the e-mail messages you sent to your classmates.

2. Previewing Before Printing

So far, you have had very limited experience sending e-mail messages. In this exercise you will get some more practice!

1. Get your new mail. You should have at least a few messages after completing Review Exercise 1.

2. Use Print Preview and Print Setup to modify and preview some aspect of the default print setup for e-mail.

3. Print the e-mail messages you received.

Assignments

1. Finding E-mail Addresses for Your Job Search

Use the Career Magazine Jobline Database to search for jobs in your area. Locate the e-mail addresses of the contact persons for those jobs. (Hint: look for text links on Web pages that are e-mail addresses.) Use a word processing application to create and print a list of the e-mail addresses you find. Be sure to include the name of the organization, the URL of the home page on which you found the e-mail address, and the e-mail address for each.

2. Requesting Application Information

Compose e-mail messages to at least four people or companies from the list you created in Assignment 1. Your e-mail messages should be inquiries about jobs or about submitting applications for jobs within their organizations. Send and print these e-mail messages.

Using Advanced E-mail Features

In Project 3, you just scratched the surface of the features Messenger has to offer for handling your e-mail. Now you will have the opportunity to explore a few more features of Netscape Communicator's e-mail component.

Objectives

After completing this project, you will be able to:

➤ **Reply to and forward e-mail**

➤ **Organize e-mail**

➤ **Use the Address Book**

➤ **Send and receive e-mail attachments**

➤ **Create links in e-mail messages**

The Challenge

Now that you have begun to use e-mail as a communication tool in your job search, you realize that you would like to know a little more about it. You wish you could organize your e-mail and sort through your e-mail lists. You also have a number of contacts you'd like to keep track of and wish there was a way to store people's names, addresses, and other important information. You wonder if Messenger has features that will help you.

The Solution

As you hoped, Messenger offers a host of features that will help you keep your communications organized. In this project, you will learn to use Messenger to organize your mail, to store the names and addresses of business contacts, and more. The first step is to learn to reply to and forward e-mail messages you have received.

Replying To and Forwarding E-mail

You will often find that you want to send replies to e-mail messages you receive. To send a reply, you could find the sender's e-mail address in the header of the message you are replying to, then select the New Message button in the Messenger message list toolbar, enter the address in the message composition window, enter a subject to jog the memory of the person to whom you are replying regarding the topic of the original message, compose your reply, and send it using the Send button. Sounds like a lot of work, doesn't it? Well, it is. That's why Netscape has provided you with a Reply button in the message list toolbar that does most of the work for you.

TASK 1: TO REPLY TO AN E-MAIL MESSAGE

 Launch Netscape Messenger.

> **Tip** Launching Netscape Messenger was covered in Project 3 beginning on page 77 if you need a refresher.

The Inbox message list window is displayed, showing the headers of all e-mail messages currently in your Messenger Inbox. If there are no messages listed, either send yourself a message or ask one of your classmates to send you a message, then select the Get Msg button to receive your new mail.

> **Tip** Sending e-mail messages using Netscape Messenger was covered in Project 3 beginning on page 87 if you need a refresher.

2 Select the header of a message to which you would like to send a reply. If displayed, select the header of a message you sent to yourself in Project 3.

3 Select the  button in the toolbar.

A pull-down menu appears showing two options, Reply to Sender and Reply to Sender and All Recipients.

Reply to Sender will address your reply message only to the sender of the original message. Reply to Sender and All Recipients will address your reply both to the sender of the orginal message and to everyone else to whom the original message was sent.

4 Choose the Reply to Sender option.

A message composition window appears. Notice that the To and Subject fields are already completed, with the sender's address and a reference to the subject of the original message. You may also see the text of the original message at the top of the message composition area preceded by "[Sender's name] wrote:".

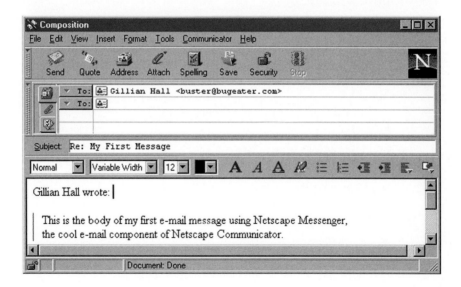

This is a feature called *quoting* which automatically includes the original message with your reply. Quoting the original message is the default preference for Messenger.

> **Tip** To enable or disable quoting, select Preferences from the Edit menu. Select the Messages panel in the Preferences window, and check or uncheck the "Automatically quote original message when replying" option. You can also use the Quote button in the message composition toolbar to manually quote a message when message quoting is disabled.

5 In the message composition area, type **This is my reply to my first e-mail message.**

6 Select the [Send] button in the toolbar.

That's all there is to it! If you have just sent a reply to a message you sent to yourself in Project 3, then wait a few seconds and use the [Get Msg] button to view your reply.

In addition to replying to e-mail messages, there may be times when you will want to forward an e-mail message you have received to someone else. This is common in business. For example, if someone sends you information you know a colleague is also interested in, or if you receive an inquiry that would be more appropriately handled by someone else in your organization, you would forward the message to the appropriate person.

Although you could forward e-mail messages by copying the header and body of the message you received and pasting it into the one you are sending, there is an easier way. Netscape Messenger provides a Forward button in the toolbar which does most of the work for you.

TASK 2: TO FORWARD AN E-MAIL MESSAGE

1 Select the header of a message that you would like to forward.

2 Select the [Forward] button in the toolbar.

A message composition window appears. Notice that the Subject field is already completed, with a reference to the subject of the original message. You have to enter the address of the recipient, and in this exercise, you will forward the message to yourself.

3 In the To field, enter your own e-mail address.

Now you can write a quick note to the person to whom you are forwarding the message.

4 In the message composition area, type **Thought you might be interested in this message!**

5 Select the [Send] button in the toolbar.

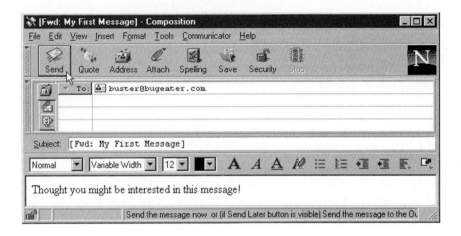

That's all there is to it! In a few seconds you can use the 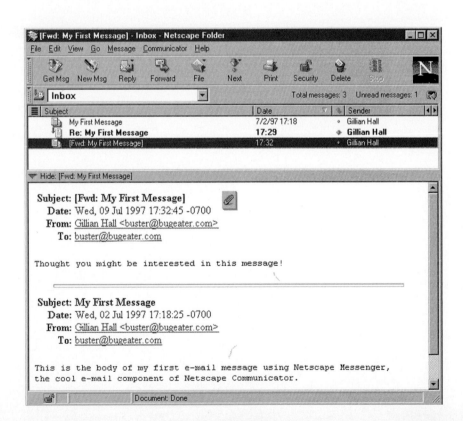 button to view your forwarded message.

6 Select the button in the message list toolbar.

Your forwarded message will be downloaded and its header displayed in the message list window.

7 Select the header of the forwarded message.

8 If it's not already displayed, open the message display area using the message display button at the bottom of the header display area.

Notice that your message is displayed first, followed by the message that you forwarded. The forwarded message is displayed complete with header so the recipient knows where the forwarded message originated, to whom it was originally sent, and when.

Organizing E-mail

As you receive more messages, you may want to organize them in some way. Netscape Messenger provides a number of ways for you to organize your e-mail. You can sort message headers or organize them into containers. One method of organizing your e-mail is by sorting message headers in the message list window.

Sorting E-mail Messages

In the message list window, you can sort e-mail message headers by any of the column headers like date, subject, sender, or status, and you can specify the sort order you prefer, ascending or decending.

In the message list window, notice the arrow in one of the column headers. In the example shown below, the arrow appears in the Date column header. This means that the message headers are currently sorted by Date. Because the arrow is pointing down, the messages are sorted in descending order with the most recent message displayed last.

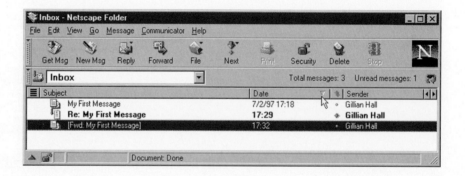

TASK 3: TO CHANGE SORT ORDER

1   In the message list window, select the column header displaying an arrow. For example, select the Date column header.

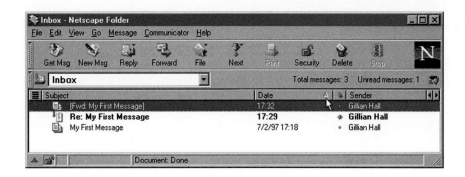

Notice that the direction of the arrow is reversed from pointing downward to pointing upward. Similarly, the sort order of the message headers is reversed, from descending to ascending.

2 Select the column header again, and the sort order returns to descending.

> **Tip** You can also change the sort order of message headers by choosing Sort from the View menu, and selecting the desired sort order option from the submenu.

TASK 4: TO SORT BY A DIFFERENT COLUMN HEADER

1 Select the Sender column header in the message list window.

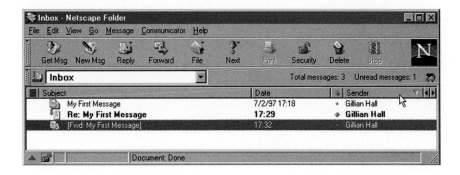

Notice that an arrow appears in the Sender column header indicating that message headers are now sorted by Sender.

> **Tip** You can sort message headers by any of the column headers simply by selecting the desired column header. Alternatively, you can use the Sort option in the View menu to select sorting preferences.

2　Choose the Sort option from the View menu.

3　Select the by Date option from the Sort submenu.

Notice that the messages are once again sorted by date and that the arrow is again displayed in the Date column header.

Using E-mail Containers

In addition to organizing your e-mail within a message list, you can create additional message lists and organize your e-mail by grouping messages into these lists or e-mail *containers*. Containers are Messenger's automatic equivalent of e-mail folders. In fact, your e-mail is already organized into several containers automatically created by Messenger.

TASK 5: TO VIEW E-MAIL CONTAINERS

1　In the message list window, select the down arrow in the container field labeled Inbox.

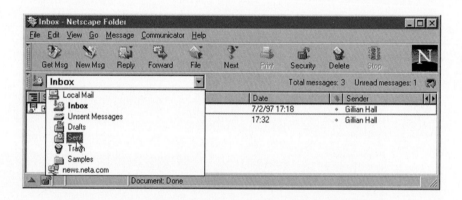

Notice that a menu drops down displaying a Local Mail container and a number of containers within the Local Mail container. Among these are the Inbox that you have been viewing.

2　Select Sent in the container list to display the headers of e-mail messages in the Sent container.

All the messages you have sent so far should appear in the message list window. Notice that the container field now contains the name of the currently displayed e-mail container, Sent.

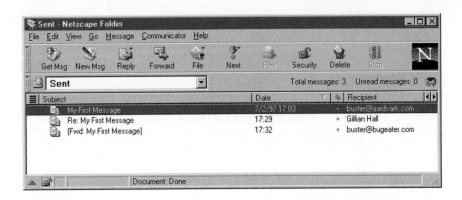

While Messenger provides a number of default e-mail containers like Inbox, Sent, and Trash, you can create your own e-mail folders and organize your mail as you please using these folders. To create your own e-mail folders you must first go to the *Message Center*, the Messenger "central post office."

TASK 6: TO GO TO THE MESSAGE CENTER

1 In the message list window, choose Local Mail from the pull-down container menu.

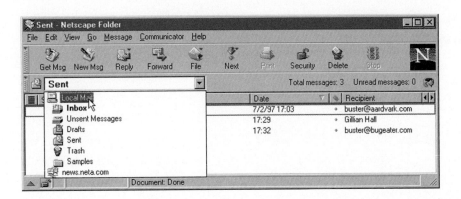

> **Tip** You can also go to the Message Center by choosing Message Center from the Communicator menu in the message list toolbar.

The Message Center window is displayed. Notice that all of the e-mail containers are listed beneath the Local Mail container. You can go to the message list window for any one of these containers by double-clicking on its icon in the list.

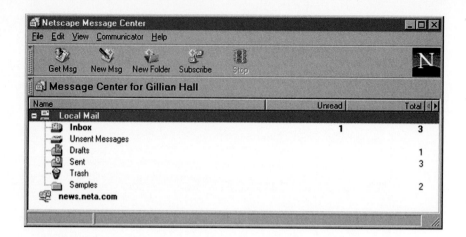

TASK 7: TO CREATE A NEW E-MAIL FOLDER

1 Select the New Folder button in the Message Center toolbar.

2 The New Folder dialog is displayed.

3 In the Name field type **Job Search Mail**

4 Select Inbox from the Create as subfolder of drop-down list.

5 Select the OK button

The new Job Search Mail folder appears as a subfolder of Inbox in the Message Center window.

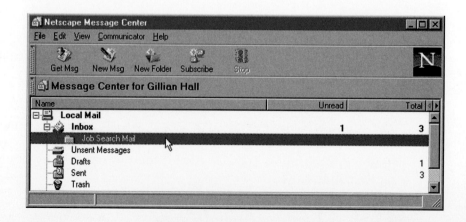

TASK 8: TO RETURN TO THE MESSAGE LIST WINDOW

1 In the Message Center window, double-click the Inbox icon.

The message list window appears displaying the Inbox message list.

TASK 9: TO FILE AN E-MAIL MESSAGE

1 Select the first e-mail message header in the Inbox message list.

2 Select the [File] button from the message list toolbar.

A pull-down menu appears displaying all of the e-mail containers.

3 Choose the Inbox menu option.

A submenu appears containing the new e-mail folder you just created.

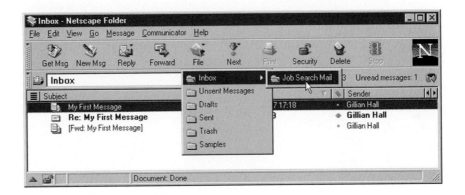

4 Select the Job Search Mail folder from the submenu.

The selected e-mail message disappears from the Inbox message list. It has been moved to the Job Search Mail folder.

5 Make the Job Search Mail message list appear by choosing it from the pull-down container menu.

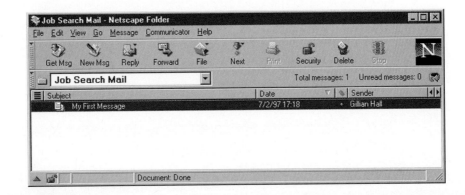

Notice that the e-mail message you selected and filed is now displayed in the Job Search Mail message list.

6 Return to the Inbox message list by choosing it from the pull-down container menu.

TASK 10: TO MOVE AN E-MAIL FOLDER

In the Message Center window, you can move any e-mail folder to a new location simply by dragging it with the mouse.

1 Use the pull-down container menu or the Communicator menu to go to the Message Center.

2 Select the Job Search Mail folder, and drag it to the Local Mail icon.

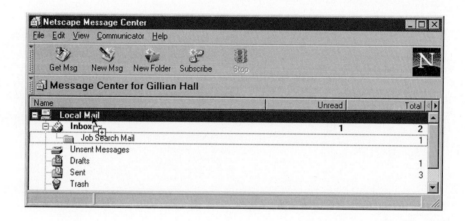

The Job Search Mail folder is now displayed as a subfolder of Local Mail rather than of Inbox.

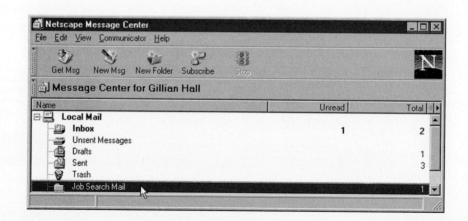

TASK 11: TO DELETE AN E-MAIL FOLDER

1 Select the Job Search Mail folder in the Message Center window.

2 Choose the Delete Folder option from the Edit menu.

The Job Search Mail folder is now displayed as a subfolder of the Trash container. The Job Search Mail folder will stay in the Trash container until you permanently delete it by deleting it from the Trash container.

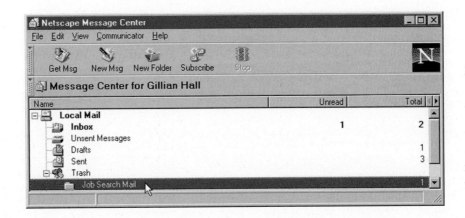

3 In the Trash container, select the Job Search Mail folder.

4 Again choose Delete Folder from the Edit menu.

A warning dialog will appear because the Job Search Mail folder is not empty.

5 Select the OK button.

The folder and its contents are permanently deleted.

Using the Address Book

When you begin receiving and sending e-mail messages on a regular basis, you will find that it becomes tedious to locate and enter the same addresses over and over when sending mail to people you correspond with often. It is for this reason that Netscape Messenger provides you with a feature called an *Address Book*. Once you have entered a name and e-mail address in your Address Book, you need never type it again. You will simply click the appropriate name and both the person's name and e-mail address are automatically entered in your message composition window.

TASK 12: TO ACCESS THE ADDRESS BOOK

1 Choose Address Book from the Communicator menu.

The Address Book window appears.

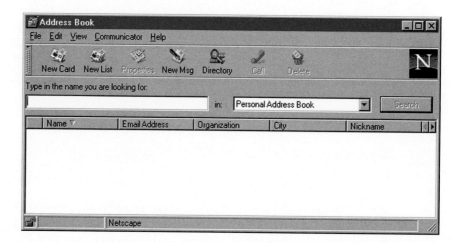

TASK 13: TO ADD AN ADDRESS

1 Choose the button in the Address Book toolbar.

A New Card window appears. Each address in your Address Book is entered on an address card. The idea is to make the Address Book feel like a traditional Rolodex or card file.

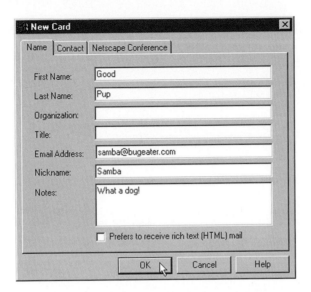

> **Tip** You can also add a new address to the Address Book by choosing New Card from the Address Book File menu.

2 Complete the New Card using the name, e-mail address, nickname, and any notes for one of your friends or classmates.

3 Select the OK button to save the address card.

Your new address card appears in the Address Book list.

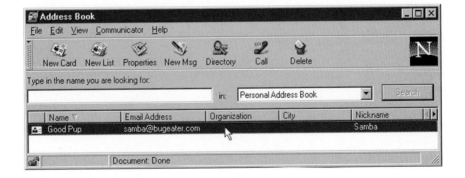

TASK 14: TO MODIFY AN ADDRESS

1 Select the address you wish to modify.

2 Select the Properties button.

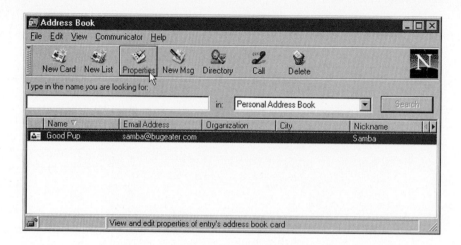

The address card appears, and you can make any desired changes to the information on the card.

> **Tip** You can also double-click an address in the Address Book list to display and modify its properties.

3 Select the [OK] button to save your changes.

TASK 15: TO DELETE AN ADDRESS

1 Select the address you wish to delete.

2 Select the [Delete] button.

The address is deleted from the Address Book list.

3 Choose Undo from the Edit menu to undelete the address.

> **Tip** You can also choose Delete from the Edit menu to delete the selected address from the Address Book list.

TASK 16: TO ADDRESS A NEW MESSAGE

1 Select an address in your Address Book list.

2 Select the [New Msg] button.

A message composition window appears. Notice that the To field is completed with the address you selected in the Address Book.

> **Tip**   You can also choose New Message from the File menu to address a new message with the selected e-mail address.

3   Close the message composition window.

Sending and Receiving E-mail Attachments

Let's say you have your resume all nicely formatted as a Microsoft Word document, and you want to send it to a prospective employer using e-mail. Rather than pasting the text of your resume into a message composition window, it would be nicer to be able to send your formatted resume file. Using Messenger, you can do just that. In addition to text messages, you can use Messenger to send and receive any type of computer file from one computer to another. When you attach a file to an e-mail message, it is called an *attachment*.

TASK 17: TO ATTACH A FILE TO AN E-MAIL MESSAGE

1   Choose Messenger Mailbox or Inbox from the Communicator menu to return to the Inbox message list window.

2   Select the New Msg button.

A message composition window appears.

3   Enter your own e-mail address in the To field.

4   In the Subject field, type **Internet Job Resouces**

5   In the message area, type **Here is a list of Internet employment resource bookmarks I've compiled for my job search.**

6   Select the Attach button.

A pull-down menu appears.

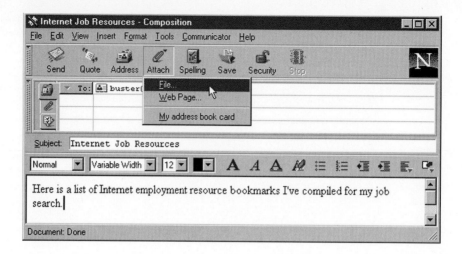

7 Choose the File option from the pull-down menu.

A window appears titled Enter file to attach. Using this window, you will select the file you wish to attach to your e-mail message. If you remember where you put it, a convenient file to send would be the bookmarks file you saved in Project 1. Otherwise, select any file you have. Just try to stick with relatively small files that won't take too long to send or receive.

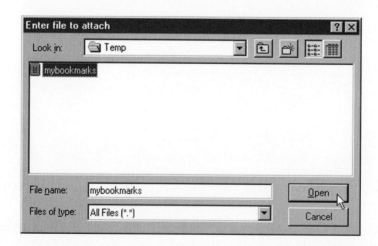

8 Choose a file to attach, and select the Open button.

The selected file name and path appear as an attachment in the message composition window. You are now ready to send your e-mail message with an attached file.

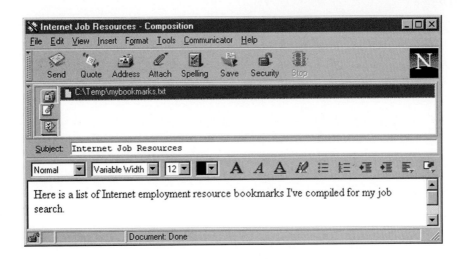

TASK 18: TO SEND A MESSAGE WITH AN ATTACHMENT

1 Select the [Send] button in the message composition window.

Your e-mail message with the attached file is sent.

TASK 19: TO RECEIVE A MESSAGE WITH AN ATTACHMENT

1 Select the [Get Mail] button in the message list window.

Your e-mail message with the attached file is downloaded. This may take a moment or two depending on the size of the attached file.

2 Select the new message, and open the message display area if necessary.

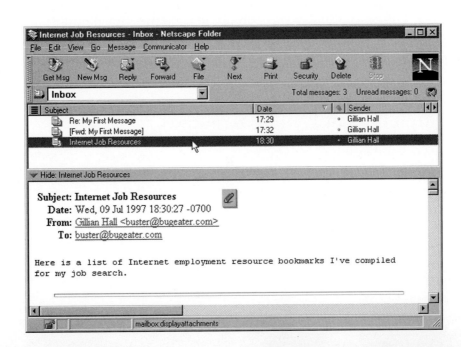

Notice the horizontal line following the text of the e-mail message. This line is a tell-tale sign of an attachment to follow.

3 Use the vertical scroll bar to scroll down to view the attached file.

If you used a bookmarks file as your attachment, then you will find a bunch of HTML code and URLs displayed, as shown below.

If you attached another type of file like a Word document, you will find a box containing the name of the file as a text link. When this text link is selected, Messenger will ask you where you would like to save the attached file, and will then write the file to the specified location.

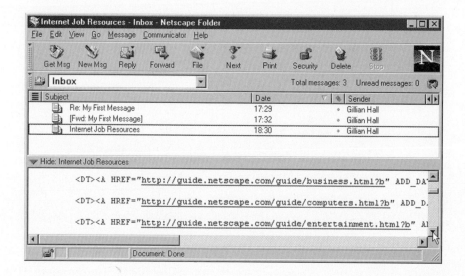

In addition to sending files as e-mail attachments, you can also use Messenger to send Web pages as e-mail attachments. To do this, you simply choose Web Page instead of file from the Attach button pull-down menu. Messenger will then ask you for the URL of the Web page you wish to send.

Creating Links in E-mail Messages

Yet another neat feature of Netscape Messenger is its ability to identify an e-mail address or a URL within the text of e-mail messages. If you receive an e-mail message containing either an e-mail address or a URL, they appear as text links when you are using Netscape Messenger.

TASK 20: TO INCLUDE A TEXT LINK IN AN E-MAIL MESSAGE

1 If it's not already displayed, choose Messenger Mailbox from the Communicator menu to return to the Inbox message list window.

2 Select the ![New Msg] button.

A message composition window appears.

3 Enter your own e-mail address in the To field.

4 In the Subject field, type **A Great Job Link**

5 In the message area, type **Check out http://www.jobweb.com for great employment opportunities via the Web!**

6 Select the ![Send] button.

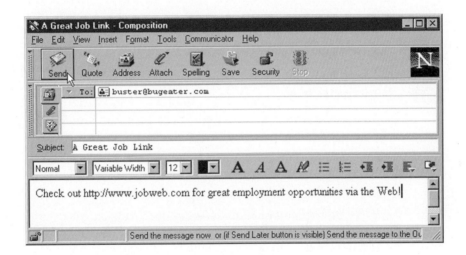

7 After your message is sent, select the ![Get Msg] button to download the message you just sent.

8 Select the new message, and open the message display area if necessary.

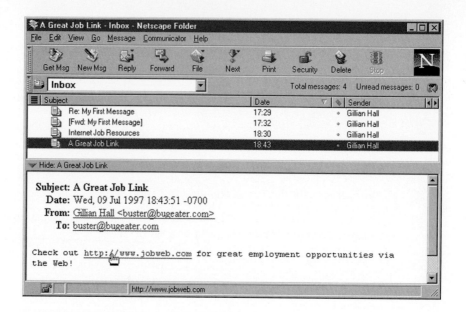

Notice that the URL you typed is now displayed as a text link.

9 Select the text link.

Netscape Navigator is launched and a browser window displays the Web page located at the given address.

> **Tip** Unfortunately, not everyone uses Netscape Messenger or an e-mail application that can "understand" URLs when it encounters them as text in an e-mail message. This means that if you send a message containing a URL, the recipient will not necessarily experience the nifty e-mail link. Ah well.

The Conclusion

In this project you have learned to use a few more of Netscape Messenger's e-mail features. While you now have an excellent grasp of e-mail and some of the tools Messenger provides to help you communicate effectively over the Internet, there remains a host of Messenger features you have not yet explored. You will have a chance to go further in your exploration of Messenger's features in the following Assignments. You may also use Netscape Communicator Online Help to learn more about the many e-mail features offered by Messenger.

This concludes Project 4. You can either exit Netscape Communicator or go on to work the Study Questions, Review Exercises, and Assignments.

Summary and Exercises

Summary

- Use the Reply button in the message list window to compose a reply to an e-mail message you received.
- Use the Forward button to forward an e-mail message to someone else.
- You can sort e-mail message headers by any of the column headers by selecting the desired column header.
- You can select between ascending and descending sort orders by selecting the desired sort order from the Sort submenu of the View menu.
- You can create your own e-mail containers, called folders, into which you can organize your e-mail.
- The Message Center is the "central post office" for e-mail on your computer.
- The Address Book allows you to store the names, addresses, and other information about Internet contacts.
- The Address Book allows you to easily address e-mail messages.
- You can use the Attach button to select a file or Web page URL to you wish to send as an attachment to an e-mail message.
- You can create a link in an e-mail message by simply typing a URL.

Key Terms and Operations

Key Terms
Address Book
attachment
containers
Message Center
quoting

Operations
reply to e-mail
forward e-mail
sort e-mail message headers
open an e-mail container
create, move, and delete an e-mail folder
open the Message Center
file e-mail messages
open the Address Book
add, delete, and modify an address
use the Address button
use the Attach button

Study Questions

Multiple Choice

1. In the Reply button pull-down menu, Reply to Sender and All Recipients sends a reply to
   a. the sender only.
   b. the sender and sends a receipt to you.
   c. the sender and to all recipients of the original message.
   d. all recipients of the original message.

2. When you forward an e-mail message, the entire message including the
_____ is sent.
   a. header.
   b. Web page.
   c. document.
   d. None of the above.

3. In the message list window, you can sort e-mail messages by clicking the
_____ you wish to use as the sort criteria.
   a. column header
   b. message
   c. button
   d. container

4. You can open the Message Center by choosing
   a. Message Center from the Communicator menu.
   b. Message Center from the Messenger menu.
   c. mail from the File menu.
   d. None of the above.

5. To create a new e-mail folder, you must be in the
   a. message list window.
   b. Message Center.
   c. Inbox.
   d. message composition window.

6. Use the _____ button in the message list window to move e-mail
messages into different e-mail containers.
   a. Save
   b. Send
   c. Directory
   d. File

7. You can move an e-mail folder by _____ it in the Message Center.
   a. selecting
   b. double-clicking
   c. dragging
   d. pasting

8. To display the properties of an address card in the Address Book, you can
   a. double-click its header.
   b. select its header and select the Properties button.
   c. choose Card Properties from the Edit menu.
   d. All of the above.

9. To create a(n) _____ in an e-mail message, you type a URL.
   a. text link
   b. picture link
   c. attachment
   d. directory

10. URLs may not be displayed as _____ by some e-mail applications.
   a. text links
   b. picture links
   c. attachments
   d. directories

Short Answer

1. Use the _____ button to send an e-mail message you have received to someone else.

2. You can automatically address an e-mail message in response to a message you have received using the _____ button.

3. An option that automatically includes the text of the original message in the reply is called _____.

4. You can sort message headers in either _____ or _____ order.

5. Message headers can be sorted by any of the message list column _____.

6. Messenger provides an e-mail container called the _____ into which your new messages are automatically placed.

7. You can create your own e-mail containers called _____.

8. You can view and organize all e-mail containers and folders using the _____ _____.

9. The _____ _____ is used to store the names, addresses, and other important information about Internet contacts.

10. You can use the _____ button to send files along with your e-mail messages.

For Discussion

1. The To field label in the message composition window is a pull-down menu containing a number of other options for addressing an e-mail message. These include Cc:, Bcc:, etc. How might these different ways of addressing a message be useful, particularly when you are sending messages to multiple recipients?

2. You have written a number of e-mail messages using Messenger. This tool could become a very important component of your business communications and your job search. Making sure that your messages are professional and typo-free may be becoming important to you. Would it be helpful to be able to spell check your e-mail messages right in Messenger? Hmm...

Review Exercises

1. Beef Up Your Address Book

In Project 3, you sent e-mail messages to at least four people or companies requesting job application information. You can now begin to build a list of job search contacts using your Address Book.

1. Use the list of e-mail addresses for potential job search contacts you created in Project 3 to create at least four new address cards in your Address Book.

2. Use the Address button in the message composition window to compose a message addressed to all of these contacts requesting job application information.

3. Print the e-mail message you send by selecting it in the Sent message list and selecting the Print button.

2. Reply with a Link

You have found a bunch of Web pages that would be useful to anyone involved in a Job Search. A handy way to share that information with others is by creating a text link in an e-mail message.

1. Reply to a message you have received from a classmate with a brief review of an employment-related Web site you have visited.

2. Include a text link to the Web page you discussed.

3. Send the message.

4. Print the e-mail message you sent by selecting it in the Sent message list and selecting the Print button.

3. Reply with a Web Page Attachment

In this project, you attached a text file to an e-mail message. As you know, you can also attach a Web page to an e-mail message.

1. Reply again to the same message you replied to in Review Exercise 2. This time, though, instead of including a link to the reviewed Web site, attach its URL using the Attach button.

2. Send the message.

3. Print the e-mail message you sent by selecting it in the Sent message list and selecting the Print button.

Assignments

1. Create a Mailing List

Use the New List button in the Address Book to create a mailing list called Employment containing all the employment contacts in your Address Book. Compose and send a message addressed to the Employment list. Print the message using the Sent message list.

2. Create a Signature File

Use the Notepad to create a signature file. A signature file can contain information about yourself, a quote that tickles you, or a link to your favorite Web site. It's entirely up to you. Save your signature file as **sigfile.txt**, and print it. Select your signature file in Messenger using the Identity Preferences screen Send a message to a classmate. Your signature should automatically appear at the end of the message. Using the Sent message list, print the message you sent.

5

Communicating with Netscape Conference

In Projects 3 and 4, you learned a lot about communicating using e-mail. Although e-mail has traditionally been the primary means of communicating over the Internet, that's all changing. In the last couple of years, Internet phones have been developed, online chat has been perfected, and collaborative tools have been developed for use over the Internet. These developments have paved the way for the introduction of *Netscape Conference*, the other Internet communication component of Netscape Communicator.

Objectives

After completing this project, you will be able to:

➤ **Configure Netscape Conference**

➤ **Make an Internet phone call**

➤ **Use the chat tool**

➤ **Use the collaborative browsing tool**

➤ **Use the file exchange tool**

➤ **Use the whiteboard tool**

The Challenge

More and more companies in all industries are looking for new employees who have experience with emerging computer and communications technologies. No matter what your industry, you are likely to receive smiles of pleasure from prospective employers when you tell them of your comfort with Internet tools such as e-mail.

Although e-mail is becoming an increasingly critical component of business communications, many companies are finding that e-mail does not meet all of their electronic communications needs. The emergence of virtual offices, telecommuting, and geographically distributed teams in business are presenting organizations with a whole new set of communications needs—needs that many companies have not yet addressed.

The Solution

Netscape Conference offers tools that seamlessly integrate your Web browser and e-mail with real-time online conferencing and collaboration tools. Netscape Conference offers the solution to many emerging electronic communications needs in business. Experience with this tool will not only give you a better understanding of the Internet and its communication possibilities, but it will also increase your marketability to companies that have acknowledged the power and importance of Internet technologies to their business.

What Is Netscape Conference?

Messenger handles a rich set of communication activities related to e-mail. And while e-mail is a tremendously valuable Internet communication tool, it is not *real time*. An e-mail conversation can go on for days—during most of that time, messages are sitting unread on your server. So in some situations, e-mail is just no substitute for an actual real-time conversation. That's where Netscape Conference comes in. Conference is a collection of five real-time Internet communication tools.

Netscape Conference allows you to place Internet "phone calls" and talk to colleagues in real time, anywhere in the world. Yes, actually talk, the kind where you speak and listen. This is particularly exciting to those of us who equate Internet communications with typing and reading.

All you need to take advantage of Conference's fully duplex voice communication (which allows speaking and listening simultaneously) is a fast connection to the Internet, a sound card, speakers, and microphone for your computer. If you care to invest in a video card and camera, you can even use Conference as a "video phone" with which you both hear and see your colleague at the other end of the line.

While voice communication is great, Conference also offers a number of real-time collaboration tools that do not require sound: the chat tool, the collaborative browsing tool, the file exchange tool, and the whiteboard tool. This means that if you don't have the hardware necesseary to experience voice communication with Conference, you can still use Conference for other types of real-time communication. In this project you'll get a taste of each of Conference's five real-time communication tools.

Getting Started with Netscape Conference

Remember that all the components of Communicator are tightly integrated, so you can easily jump from one to another almost without noticing! Therefore, there are a couple of ways to launch Netscape Conference: You can first launch any other Communicator component such as Navigator, and then choose Conference from the Communicator menu.

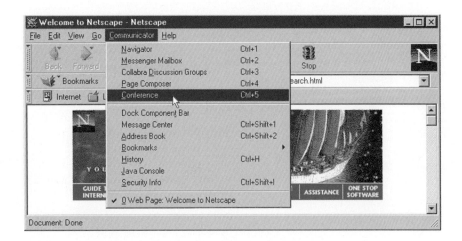

Alternatively, depending upon the way in which Netscape Communicator is installed at your school, you may be able to launch Netscape Conference directly from the Windows 95 start menu.

TASK 1: TO LAUNCH NETSCAPE CONFERENCE

1 Click the Start button ![Start] and point to Programs.

2 Point to the Netscape Communicator folder and then to Netscape Conference in the pull-down menus.

126

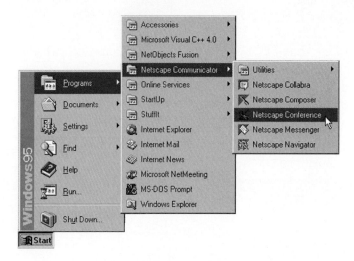

The Netscape Conference program is launched.

Just as when you launch Navigator, the Netscape Communicator startup screen appears and remains on your screen while your computer establishes its connection to the network.

The startup screen disappears when a network connection has been confirmed. It is replaced by a Netscape Conference main window.

Tip If this is the first time Conference has been launched, you will first see the Conference Setup Wizard, which will ask you a number of questions that will allow you to use the Conference communication tools to collaborate with other Conference users. Your instructor will guide you through the Setup Wizard, if needed.

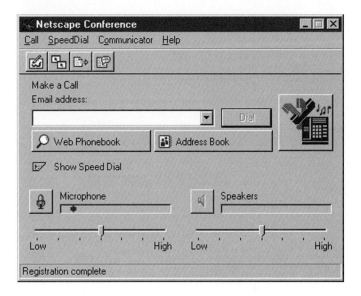

Unless you have already configured Conference using the Setup Wizard, you will need to identify yourself in the Conference Preferences window before placing your first call. This allows Conference to announce you by name to the people you call.

By registering your IP address on a ***dynamic lookup service (DLS)*** server, Conference also allows others to find you—wherever you are at the moment—with just your e-mail address. The DLS server, of course, also allows you to find other people based upon their e-mail addresses.

Without a DLS server, you would need a person's IP address to place a call to them—not an appetizing idea—especially for people who use different computers from time to time or who dial in from home. Those people have a different IP address each time they use Conference.

TASK 2: TO CONFIGURE CONFERENCE

1   Choose Preferences from the Call menu in the Conference window.

The Conference Preferences window appears displaying the Network tab. Notice that the Network tab is selected by default. The Communicator default DLS server's address is displayed, as is the address of the default Internet "phonebook" and the type of network connection you are using.

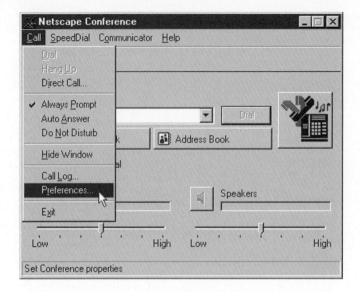

2 Select the Business Card tab in the Preferences window.

The Business Card tab is displayed. This is the screen where you will identify yourself with your name and e-mail address, as shown in the example
below.

3 Type your name in the Name field.

4 Type your e-mail address in the e-mail field.

5 Select the OK button.

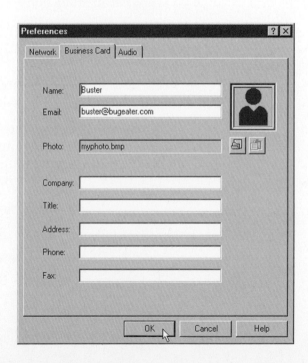

Using the Voice Conferencing Tool

Now that you have launched and configured Netscape Conference, you are ready to experience Conference's *voice conferencing tool*. For the balance of this project, you will need a partner to call who will be able to call you. Team up with one of your classmates, exchange e-mail addresses, decide which one of you will place the call and which will recieve it, and either set up a time when you will call each other, or the two of you can go ahead and begin now in your computer lab. To experience both receiving and placing a call with Conference, you and your classmate may want to go through some parts of this project twice, alternating your roles.

TASK 3: TO PLACE A CALL WITH CONFERENCE

1 In the field labeled Email address, type the e-mail address of one of your classmates who is currently using Netscape Conference.

2 Select the [Dial] button.

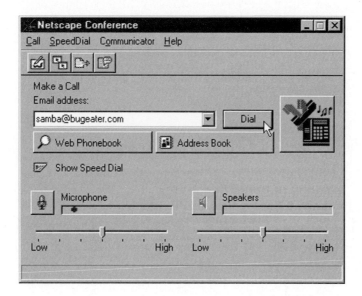

Conference then looks up the e-mail address you entered on the DLS server specified in the Conference Preferences screen. If the e-mail address is listed on the DLS server, Conference announces that it is "dialing."

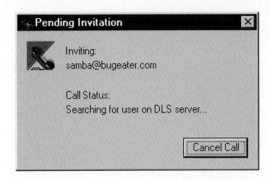

To receive your call, the recipient must be running Netscape Conference configured with his or her e-mail address and name. If this is the case, the person you are calling will see a dialog announcing that you are calling.

In addition, both you and the person you are calling will hear a telephone ringing sound.

If the person you are calling accepts your call, your Dial button ⬚ Dial will change to a Hang Up buton Hang Up .

Assuming your computer is properly equipped with a sound card, microphone, and speakers, you will hear the recipient say "Hello!"

> **Tip** If the person you are calling is already holding a conversation with someone else, if the person refuses your call, or if his or her e-mail address is not currently registered on the DLS server, then you will see a dialog explaining why your call didn't go through. In this case, you may try calling someone else, or you can leave a voice mail message when prompted.

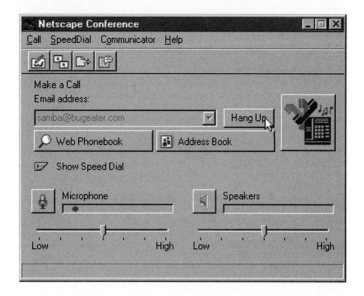

3 Try to hold a conversation with the person you have called.

4 When you have completed your call, select the Hang Up button.

> **Tip** If you are in the same room with the person you have called, as
> may be the case if you are working in a computer lab, you may actu-
> ally be able to observe firsthand the time delay involved in transmit-
> ting your voice electronically across the Internet to the call recipient's
> computer. Depending upon the speed of your respective Internet con-
> nections, this delay may be quite noticeable. A slow Internet connec-
> tion may also make your voices difficult to understand.

Using Voice Conferencing with Other Tools

A powerful feature of Netscape Conference is that it allows you to carry
on a voice dialog with the other party while you are using other Conference collaboration tools. If your computer is equipped for sound and you
have been successful in using voice conferencing, you can continue to
talk with the other party on the Conference call while using the chat, collaborative browsing, file exchange, and whiteboard tools. So don't forget
to use your voice communication capabilities to coordinate your activities
in the following sections!

Using the Chat Tool

Hopefully, you have now experienced a successful voice phone call using Netscape Conference. Even if your computer is not configured for sound, you can still use Conference to place and receive phone calls—you just won't be able to actually speak with the person you call. If this is the case, if you wish to communicate silently, or if you wish to collaborate in real time on a text document, then the Conference *chat tool* is for you.

TASK 4: TO OPEN THE CHAT TOOL

1 If you are not currently engaged in a Conference phone call, dial a classmate now by his or her e-mail address in the E-mail address field and selecting the ▢ Dial ▢ button. Or, wait to receive a call from a classmate.

2 After you are connected, select the chat button 🗏

The Conference Text Chat window appears.

TASK 5: TO "CHAT" USING THE CHAT TOOL

1 Type a greeting in the Personal Note Pad.

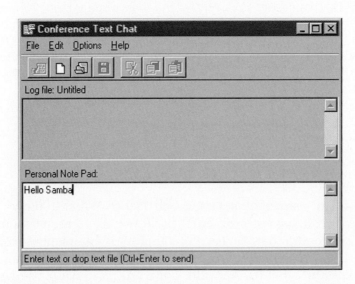

2 Press (CONTROL) + (ENTER), or select the Send button 🗏 to send your message.

Your sent message is posted in the Log file.

When your message is answered, the answer will also appear in the Log file.

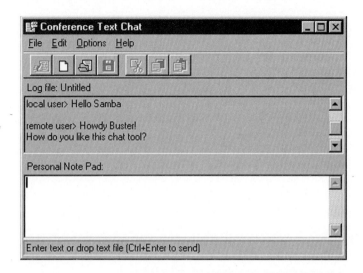

3   Use the chat tool to continue your conversation

When you are finished conversing using the chat tool, you can print your conversation log.

TASK 6: TO PRINT YOUR CONVERSATION

1   Choose Print from the File menu.

2   Select the   OK   button on the Print dialog that appears.

TASK 7: TO CLOSE THE CHAT TOOL

1   Choose Close from the File menu.

Using the Collaborative Browsing Tool

In addition to talking and online "chatting," Conference also allows you to communicate in other ways. The *collaborative browsing tool* allows you to take control of another person's Navigator Web browser to display and discuss material available on the Web.

TASK 8: TO OPEN THE COLLABORATIVE BROWSING TOOL

1 If you are not currently engaged in a Conference phone call, dial a classmate now by typing his or her e-mail address in the E-mail address field and selecting the [Dial] button. Or, wait to receive a call.

2 After you are connected, select the collaborative browsing button 🔲

The Conference Collaborative Browsing window appears.

TASK 9: TO START A COLLABORATIVE BROWSING SESSION

1 Select the [Start Browsing] button to begin a collaborative browsing session.

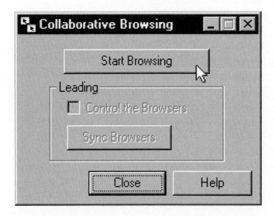

The person you are connected with will see a dialog announcing that you are starting a collaborative browsing session.

If they choose to join, then both your Navigator windows will open.

By default, the person initiating the collaborative browsing session is the one who will lead. Therefore, you are the leader and are now in control of the session. You can relinquish control, though, by unchecking the Control the Browsers box in the Conference Collaborative Browsing window.

TASK 10: TO LEAD A COLLABORATIVE BROWSING SESSION

1 Type a URL in the Navigator location field, and press (ENTER)

Navigator will display the designated Web page both in your browser window and in the browser window of the other person involved in the collaborative browsing session.

2 Select a link on the Web page displayed, and you will continue to lead both Web browsers.

TASK 11: TO END A COLLABORATIVE BROWSING SESSION

1 When you are finished with your collaborative browsing session, close or hide the Navigator window, and display the Conference Collaborative Browsing window.

2 Select the ⌑ Stop Browsing ⌑ button.

The collaborative browsing session is terminated. The Conference call, however, remains connected until you hang up using the Conference window.

TASK 12: TO CLOSE THE COLLABORATIVE BROWSING TOOL

1 Select the ⌑ Close ⌑ button in the Collaborative Browsing window.

Using the File Exchange Tool

In Project 4 you learned to exchange files using e-mail attachments with Messenger. The Conference *file exchange tool* offers an alternative means of sending and receiving files over the Internet.

TASK 13: TO OPEN THE FILE EXCHANGE TOOL

1 If you are not currently engaged in a Conference phone call, dial a classmate now by typing his or her e-mail address in the Email address field and selecting the | Dial | button. Or, wait to receive a call from a classmate.

2 After you are connected, select the file exchange button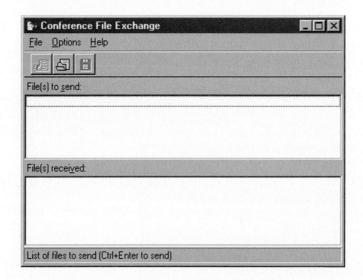

The Conference File Exchange window appears.

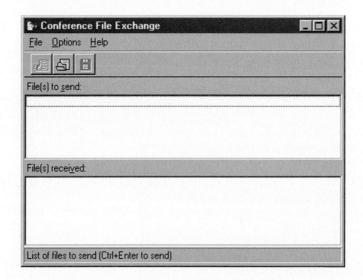

TASK 14: TO SELECT A FILE TO SEND

1 Select the [🖫] button in the Conference File Exchange window to select a file to send.

The Add File to Send List dialog appears. You can now select a file to send. This can be any file, but try to keep it on the small side so that the transfer won't take too long. Try sending a small word processor document like the the list of e-mail addresses you created in Project 3 or the e-mail signature file you created in Project 4.

2 Select a file to send.

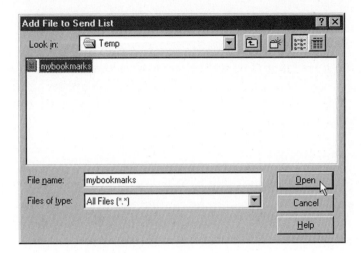

3   Select the [Open] button.

The selected file is displayed as a file to send in the Conference File Exchange window.

4   Select the send file button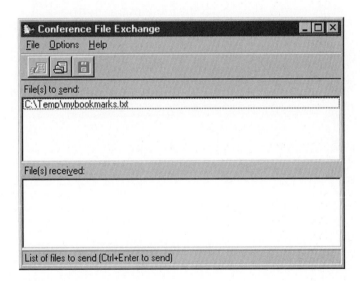

The file is sent to the person(s) with whom you are connected. Received files appear in each of their Conference File Exchange windows. Received files can be saved using the Save option in the File menu.

TASK 15: TO CLOSE THE FILE EXCHANGE TOOL

1   Choose Close from the File menu in the Conference File Exchange window.

Using the Whiteboard Tool

The last of the communications tools offered by Netscape Conference is the **whiteboard tool**. This tool allows you to open, share, and interactively edit and mark up image files. The whiteboard supports a number of popular graphics formats and is even capable of capturing images from the Windows 95 desktop.

When an image file has been imported by one of the parties involved in the Conference call, both parties see the image in their Whiteboard window. The Whiteboard window can then be synchronized to make sure that both parties involved in the Conference call are seeing the same thing as the image is marked up and edited using the whiteboard drawing tools. If no image is loaded, the drawing tools can be used to actually create image and text elements on the screen in an online collaborative fashion.

TASK 16: TO OPEN THE WHITEBOARD TOOL

1 If you are not currently engaged in a Conference phone call, dial a classmate now by typing that person's e-mail address in the Email address field and selecting the Dial button. Or, wait to receive a call.

2 After you are connected, select the whiteboard button

The Whiteboard window appears on your screen. After a brief delay, the Whiteboard window will also appear on the other party's screen as well.

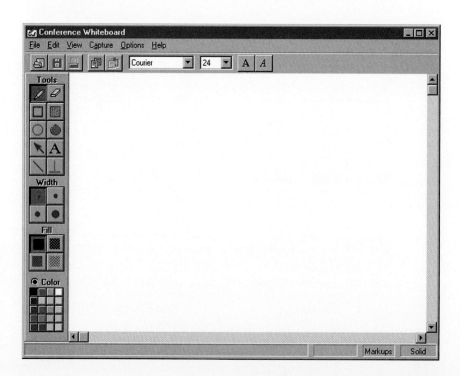

TASK 17: TO USE THE TEXT TOOL

1 Select the text tool [A] in the Tools palette.

2 Select the point in the Whiteboard window where you would like to begin entering text.

3 Type some text.

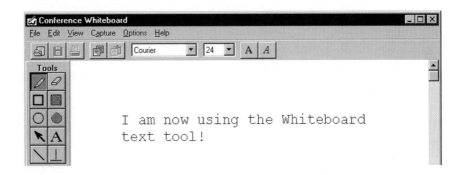

As with any action, the text you typed appears in both your and the other party's Whiteboard window.

TASK 18: TO USE THE RECTANGLE TOOL

1 Select the rectangle tool [□] in the Tools palette.

2 Select a point just above and to the left of the text you entered.

3 Drag down and to the right, creating a box around the text.

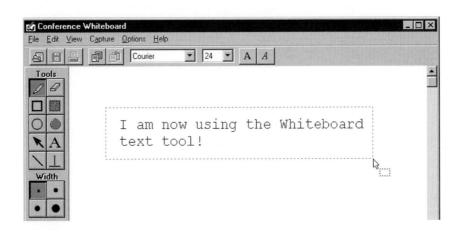

The whiteboard tools palette provides free-form pen, eraser, rectangle, filled rectangle, circle, filled circle, pointer, text, and line tools.

TASK 19: TO USE THE OTHER DRAWING TOOLS

1 Select desired tools, line widths, fills, and colors from the whiteboard palettes, and collaborate with the other party on the call to continue building the image in the Whiteboard window.

When you are finished with your collaborative drawing, you can print it. You can also save it to a file that can then be loaded into the whiteboard later.

TASK 20: TO PRINT THE WHITEBOARD

1 Select the Print button in the Whiteboard window.

2 Select the OK button on the Print dialog that appears.

TASK 21: TO CLEAR THE WHITEBOARD

1   Choose Clear Whiteboard from the Edit menu.

Your drawing is cleared from the whiteboard. Now that you have a feeling for the drawing tools in the whiteboard, you are ready to load and mark up a graphic image.

TASK 22: TO CLOSE THE WHITEBOARD TOOL

1   Choose Close from the File menu in the Conference Whiteboard window.

The Conclusion

In this project you have learned to use a few more of Netscape Messenger's e-mail features. While you now have an excellent grasp of e-mail and some of the tools Messenger provides to help you communicate effectively over the Internet, there remains a host of Messenger features you have not yet explored. You will have a chance to go further in your exploration of Messenger's features in the following Assignments. You may also use Netscape Communicator Online Help to learn more about the many e-mail features offered by Messenger.

This concludes Project 5. You can either exit Netscape Communicator or go on to work the Study Questions, Review Exercises, and Assignments.

Summary and Exercises

Summary

- Netscape Conference is an Internet tool used for real-time communication and collaboration.
- Start Conference by selecting Conference from the Communicator menu.
- Conference must be configured with your name and e-mail address before you can use it to place a call.
- When you launch Conference, you are registered in the dynamic lookup service (DLS) server.
- The DLS server allows you to place Internet calls to other Conference users.
- You can place a call using Conference by entering the e-mail address of the person you are trying to reach.
- You can communicate by voice while using other Conference tools.
- The Conference chat tool is used to hold an online meeting, to collaborate on a text document, or to generate real-time meeting notes.
- Collaborative browsing allows you to lead the browsers of other people on the Conference call.
- The Conference file exchange tool allows you to send and receive files over the Internet.
- The Conference whiteboard tool allows you to edit and mark up graphic files or to create graphics collaboratively with other people on the Conference call.

Key Terms and Operations

Key Terms
chat tool
collaborative browsing tool
dynamic lookup service (DLS)
file exchange tool
Netscape Conference
voice conferencing tool
whiteboard tool

Operations
launch Netscape Conference
configure Conference
place a call
use voice conferencing
open the chat tool
send and receive chat messages
print a chat log
close the chat tool
open the collaborative browsing tool
lead a collaborative browsing session
close the collaborative browsing tool
open the file exchange tool
send a file
close the file exchange tool
open the whiteboard tool
use whiteboard text and drawing tools
print the whiteboard
clear the whiteboard
close the whiteboard

Study Questions _____

Multiple Choice

1. To start Netscape Conference, you can choose Conference from the
   _____ menu.
   a. Go
   b. Communicator
   c. Window
   d. View

2. When Conference is launched, your e-mail address and IP address are
   registered on the specified _____ server.
   a. POP
   b. SMTP
   c. DLS
   d. IP

3. You can use an e-mail address or _____ address to place a call
   using Conference.
   a. HTTP
   b. IP
   c. URL
   d. FTP

4. You can use _____ simultaneously with other Conference
   tools.
   a. the whiteboard
   b. the chat tool
   c. collaborative browsing
   d. voice conferencing

5. The chat tool allows you to conduct a real-time _____
   conversation.
   a. voice
   b. graphical
   c. text
   d. fully duplex sound

6. To generate meeting notes, you can print the chat _____
   a. log file.
   a. window.
   a. note pad.
   a. None of the above.

7. With the _____ tool, you can control another person's
   Navigator window.
   a. whiteboard
   b. file exchange
   c. collaborative browsing
   d. chat

8. The _____ tool is used to send and receive files.
   a. whiteboard
   b. file exchange
   c. collaborative browsing
   d. chat

9. The whiteboard tool allows you to open, share, and interactively create, edit and mark up _____ files.
   a. text
   b. sound
   c. movie
   d. image

10. The whiteboard offers a number of _____ tools.
    a. drawing
    b. online chat
    c. word processing
    d. sound editing

Short Answer

1. Conference's voice conferencing is _____, which allows you to speak and listen simultaneously.

2. _____ communication means that you and another party can converse and collaborate online without long delays.

3. In order to use Conference for voice communication, your computer must be equipped with a sound card, speakers, and _____.

4. You can start Conference either from the Communicator menu or using the Windows 95 _____ menu.

5. Before you can use Conference to place a call, Conference's _____ preferences must be properly configured.

6. A dynamic lookup service allows you to call other Conference users with just their _____ address.

7. You can call someone who is not registered on a DLS server by entering their _____ address.

8. Like attaching a file to an e-mail message using Messenger, you can send and receive files with Conference using the _____ tool.

9. To start a collaborative browsing session during a Conference call, you must open the collaborative browsing tool and select the _____ button.

10. You can elect to lead a collaborative browsing session by selecting the _____ check box in the Collaborative Browsing window.

For Discussion

1. Like Netscape Messenger, Conference allows you to communicate over the Internet. What are the advantages that Conference offers over Messenger? What are the advantages of Messenger?

2. Coordinating teams whose members may work in different locations is a major challenge for business today. What are some ways that Conference can be used to address this issue?

Review Exercises

1. Discuss a Task

In this project you used the whiteboard tool to markup an imported image and to use the drawing tools to create your own image. Now you will use the chat tool to make plans regarding an image you will create collaboratively using the whiteboard tool.

1. Place a call to one of your classmates using Conference.

2. Use the chat tool to discuss and decide on an image you want to create (e.g., a schematic of your computer lab, an organization chart, a picture of a house, etc).

3. Print the chat tool log file.

2. Perform a Task

You have used Conference's chat tool to decide what image you will create. Now you can use the whiteboard to collaborate on creating the image!

1. If you are not already on the line with that person, place a call to the same person as in Review Exercise 1.

2. Open the whiteboard tool and begin to create the image you discussed in Review Exercise 1. Remember to collaborate!

3. Print the image.

Assignments

1. SpeedDial

Although the Address Book provides a convenient method for placing calls, you may have a few people that you call very frequently. Conference offers a Speed-Dial feature for recording the e-mail addresses of those people. Use the SpeedDial feature to configure at least two SpeedDial numbers and place calls using the SpeedDial feature. Don't forget Conference online help if you need assistance!

2. Send Voice Mail

If you try to place a call to someone who is not available to take your call, Conference will ask if you would like to leave voice mail for that person. Voice mail is an audio file that you record and send using Conference. When the recipient receives the voice mail message using Messenger, Conference plays it back. Record and send a voice mail message to a classmate.

6

PROJECT

Using Other Internet Resources

You have come a long way since beginning this book. You are now an accomplished Web surfer. You have organized yourself on the Web with bookmarks, performed Internet searches using a variety of tools, and have even set yourself up to use e-mail, voice communications, and collaborative tools with Netscape Communicator. The Internet offers a number of other information and communication resources, though, that you have not yet seen.

Objectives

After completing this project, you will be able to:

➤ **Understand the terms Gopher, FTP, and newsgroup**

➤ **Access Gopher servers and search Gopherspace**

➤ **Access and use FTP servers**

➤ **Configure Netscape Collabra for news**

➤ **Participate in newsgroups**

The Challenge

So far the Internet has provided some very powerful tools for your job search—the World Wide Web, e-mail, voice communication, and real-time collaboration. But you have learned that the Web and e-mail are just segments of the Internet. Are there other Internet resources out there that you have not yet explored? If there are, could they too be valuable assets in your job search?

The Solution

Now it is time to explore some other Internet resources that might also be useful in your job search. You've heard of these resources—Gopher, FTP, newsgroups—but do you really know what they are and what they're for? In this project you'll use Netscape Navigator 4.0 to find out.

URLs Revisited

Remember in Project 1 when we talked about URLs and what the different parts of URLs mean? In that discussion we introduced the idea of a protocol, which tells Netscape the document type and how to interpret the document.

So far you have seen only one type of Internet document, a Web page. All Web pages must be interpreted by Navigator using a protocol called HTTP, or Hypertext Transfer Protocol. So the URL of every Web page begins with http: to tell your Web browser that the document is a Web page and to interpret it using HTTP.

In Project 1 you also learned that the Web is just one segment of the Internet. As you know, the Internet is much older than the Web, and there is a lot of information on the Internet that is not part of the Web. So what is this other information? You will know it when you see it, because the URL will give it away! As shown in Table 7.1, different types of Internet documents are indicated by different protocols. Web pages use http:, Gopher documents use gopher:, and FTP documents use ftp:.

Table 7.1   A Few Internet Document Types

Document Type	Protocol and URL Format
FTP	ftp://*domain.name/complete.file.name*
Gopher	gopher://*domain.name:port*
Web pages	http://*domain.name/directory/path/filename.html*

Being able to distinguish different types of Internet documents by their URLs is a good start. Now let's find out just what a Gopher document is and how you can access one.

Introducing Gopher

We will begin our exploration of other Internet resources with **Gopher**. The development of Gopher by the University of Minnesota actually laid the groundwork for the philosophy behind the Web—the philosophy of making Internet resources accessible to "the rest of us."

Gopher uses a hierarchical network of menus to guide you to text-based resources located on **Gopher servers** all over the world. You can enter **Gopherspace** (the world of all Gopher servers) at any level of any Gopher menu and get anywhere—literally. It's just a matter of navigating upward and downward through the great labyrinth of menus and submenus sometimes called Gopher burrows.

For many years, Gopher offered the easiest access available to the Internet. However, in recent years Gopher has been left behind by the World Wide Web. The problem is that, while a tremendous amount of information still resides exclusively in Gopherspace, fewer and fewer people are accessing that information because, well… the Web is more fun! In fact, according to some Internet veterans, Gopher is terminally ill. Some say that Gopher is dead, while others insist that Gopher is being reincarnated in the form of super-Web pages. These new Web pages will contain the Web's equivalent of Gopher menus—lists of text links.

Using Navigator to Tunnel through Gopherspace

To access Gopher servers using Netscape Navigator 4.0, you must have two things: you must have Navigator running, and you need the address (URL) of a Gopher server. So open Navigator (if you need help with this, review the procedure for starting Netscape Communicator in the Overview). Since you may not know any Gopher server addresses off the top of your head, we'll give you one. (Let's hope that the address we give you is still valid when you read this book!)

TASK 1: TO ENTER GOPHERSPACE

 In the Navigator Location field, type **gopher://gopher.harvard.edu** and press (ENTER)

Harvard University's Gopher Menu page is displayed. That's all there is to it. You are now officially in Gopherspace. And from here you can go anywhere else in Gopherspace using the menu items displayed.

Notice the different types of icons in the Gopher Menu page. The document icon (🗅) indicates a link to a text-based document and the folder (🗀) icon indicates a link to yet another Gopher Menu page. You may also see an icon shaped like a pair of binoculars. This icon indicates a link to a Gopherspace index or a Gopher search tool.

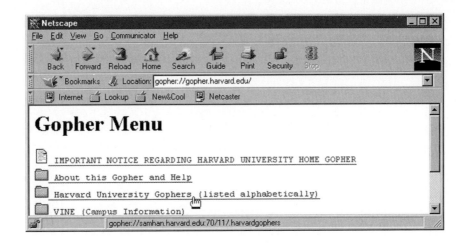

2 Scroll through the Gopher Menu page to view all the subjects available on Harvard's Gopher server.

3 Select one of the Gopher folder menu items to view the submenu for that item.

4 Use the [Back] button to return to the main Gopher menu.

TASK 2: TO VIEW A DOCUMENT ON A GOPHER SERVER

1 If this link is displayed, select <u>IMPORTANT NOTICE REGARDING HARVARD UNIVERSITY HOME GOPHER</u>

The linked text document is displayed. You can print this document, save it as text, or simply read it on the screen. Notice that this document explains that Harvard is moving its Gopher resources to the Web.

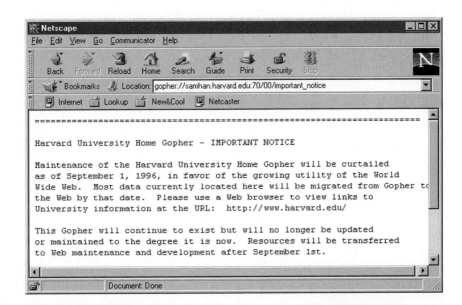

Introducing FTP

Now we will shift gears and go from Gopher to *File Transfer Protocol (FTP)*. Very simply, FTP is a means by which computers communicate with one another and exchange files. At one time, long ago, FTP involved lots of typing and lots of frustration. Luckily for all of us, those days are long past, and Netscape now provides one of the easiest FTP interfaces around.

You can use FTP to retrieve files and transmit files virtually anywhere in the world. FTP has revolutionized the ease with which we can obtain goodies from the Internet like software updates, shareware programs, sounds, pictures, government forms, movies, and so on. FTP has also made sending files easier than it has ever been before.

What Is an FTP Server?

FTP servers are computers on the Internet set up to send and receive files using the File Transfer Protocol. FTP server administrators, select which directories can be accessed, which files can be downloaded, and into which directories users can upload (or place) files. Some FTP servers require special passwords for either download or upload access. All of these issues are determined by the FTP server administrator.

Unlike Gopher servers, FTP servers are a thriving dynamic force on the Internet. Companies and even individuals are setting up FTP servers at the pace fax machines were being set up in the 1980s. FTP servers allow companies to provides customers with all kinds of documentation online. They also facilitate data sharing between individuals. For example, the author and publishers of this book utilized FTP constantly, passing projects back and forth between Arizona and Massachusettes for revisions and review.

Using Navigator to Access FTP Servers

To access FTP servers, you need an FTP server address. Once again, we will provide you with an address, but you won't get as much mileage out of it as you did the Gopher address. Unlike Gophers, FTP servers contain no links to other FTP servers. Each FTP server is basically on its own. You can get to it if you know the address or stumble upon a link to it on a Web page. But once you get to an FTP server, you can only poke around on that FTP server. You cannot jump to some other FTP server unless you know its address too.

TASK 3: TO ACCESS AN FTP SERVER

1 In the Location field type **ftp://ftp.fedworld.gov**, and press ⏎ENTER

This is the address of the FTP server of (oh dear) the Internal Revenue Service (IRS). The IRS FTP server directories are displayed.

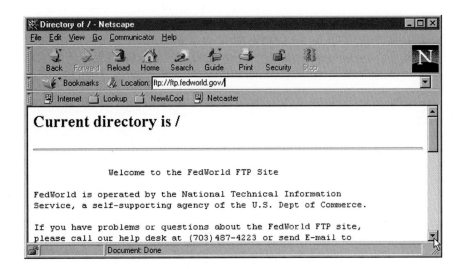

It doesn't get much easier than that. You have officially arrived at your first FTP server. From here you can explore the resources the IRS has put at your disposal.

TASK 4: TO GET AROUND ON AN FTP SERVER

1 Scroll down to display the <u>pub/</u> text link on the IRS FTP server.

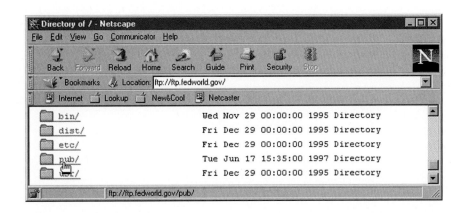

Notice that Netscape displays the FTP server using folder icons (📁) for directories. There are also special icons for documents and executable files (programs), which you will see shortly. The names of directories are displayed as text links. When you select one of these text links, the contents of the directory will be displayed.

2 Select the pub/ text link.

Most FTP servers have a pub directory that normally stores interesting information. The contents of the pub directory are displayed.

Notice that the current directory name (and its path) are always displayed at the top of the screen as the title. Notice too that you can go back up the hierarchy of directories using the Up to higher-level directory text link. These are standard features of FTP servers when they are displayed using Netscape.

3 Scroll down through the list of directories displayed, and select the irs-ps/ directory when you come to it.

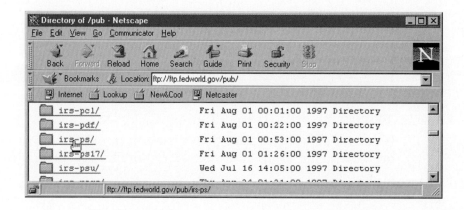

The pub/irs-ps directory of the IRS FTP server is displayed. Notice that program files and text files are displayed with special icons.

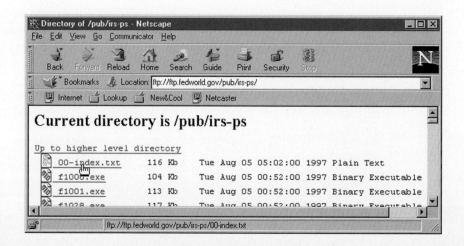

Care to guess what types of files this directory contains? That's right, tax forms. This is a useful FTP site around tax time. Rather than running to your local government office, fighting crowds, and standing in lines, you can download all the tax forms you've ever dreamed of using the IRS FTP server.

TASK 5: TO VIEW A FILE ON AN FTP SERVER:

1 In the pub/irs-ps directory, select the file called 00-index.txt.

The file called 00-index.txt is displayed on your screen. This file contains a listing of the contents of the pub/irs-ps directory and a brief description of each file.

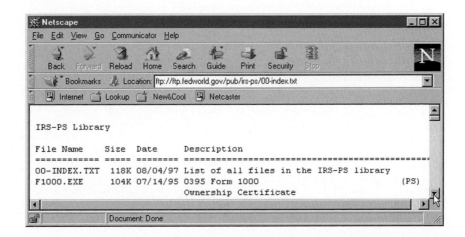

2 Scroll down through the index file until you find the description of the 1040EZ form (the description should read something like "199X Form 1040EZ").

3 Look at the file name corresponding to the description—probably F1040EZ.EXE.

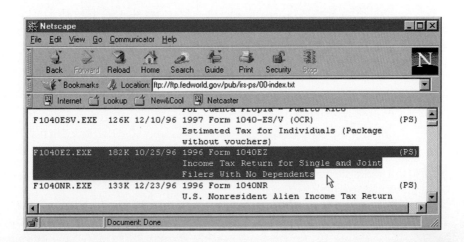

154

4 Use the Back button to return to the <u>pub/irs-ps</u> directory.

TASK 6: TO DOWNLOAD A FILE FROM AN FTP SERVER

1 Scroll down through the contents of the <u>pub/irs-ps</u> directory until you come to <u>f1040ez.exe</u>

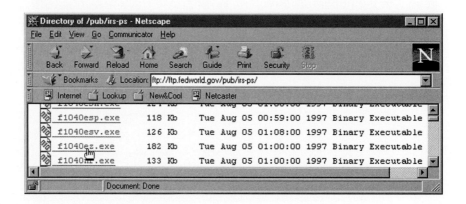

2 Select the file <u>f1040ez.exe</u>

The standard Windows Save As dialog box appears.

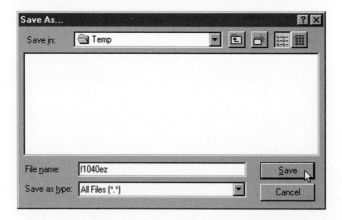

You have just initiated your first FTP file transfer. You are now going to ***download*** an electronic version of the 1040EZ tax form. ***Downloading*** a file means copying it from a remote computer to a disk on your computer.

3 Using the Save in list in the Save As dialog box, select a location in which to save the file <u>f1040ez.exe</u>

4 Select the Save button.

The Saving Location dialog box appears, and the FTP file transfer begins.

The Saving Location dialog box tells you the name of the file being downloaded, the location where it is being saved, the size of the file, the elapsed time, and the estimated time for completing the download. When the download is complete, this dialog box will disappear.

The file you just downloaded from the IRS FTP server is in a special format. It is ***archived***, or ***compressed***, to make it faster to download. Archived files are generally what we call ***self-extracting*** files. This means that the instructions needed for decompressing the file have been included with the file itself. When opened, a self-extracting archived file will write a decompressed version of the file to the same directory where the archived file resides. Receiving archived or compressed files is almost standard in the world of FTP. No one wants to wait twice as long to download a file that could have arrived in half the time if it had been compressed.

TASK 7: TO USE A DOWNLOADED FILE

1 Select Run from the Windows 95 Start menu.

The Run dialog appears.

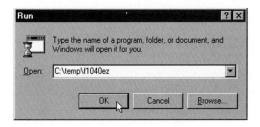

2 In the Open field, type the path and name of the file you just downloaded as shown in the example above.

A Microsoft Disk Operating System (MS/DOS) Prompt window appears, and the file automatically extracts or decompresses.

The decompressed file is written to the same location as the downloaded file and is called f1040ez.ps. The .ps file extension indicates the file type. In this case, the file is in a special format called PostScript (.ps). If you would like, you can now print the file using a DOS command. Notice, that instructions for printing the file are provided in the MS-DOS Prompt window. Let's give it a try.

3   Open a new MS-DOS Prompt window by selecting MS-DOS Prompt from the Programs submenu of the Windows 95 Start menu. Ask your instructor for help if necessary.

To print the downloaded Postscript file, your computer must be connected to a Postscript printer. To print the file, you will use a DOS command in the following format: copy filename printer, where filename is the path and name of the file (e.g., c:\temp\f1040ez.ps), and printer is the name of the port to which the desired printer is connected (e.g., lpt1).

In this case, the DOS command will be copy c:\temp\f1040ez.ps lpt1. Your instructor can help you with this step if you need assistance.

4   At the DOS prompt type **copy c:\temp\f1040ez.ps lpt1**

Confirm the printer port (lpt1) with your instructor. If instructed to do so, you may need do substitute lpt1 with another port (for example, lpt2).

5   Press ⟨ENTER⟩

The file is sent to the printer, and in a few moments you will be in possession of an official 1040EZ tax form!

6 After the form has printed, you can close both open MS-DOS Prompt windows.

Searching for FTP Servers Using the Web

These days the Web is really the best choice if you want to search for resources on the Internet. Archie is rapidly being abandoned in favor of friendlier, faster, easier methods for performing FTP searches. In fact, you can easily locate FTP servers for most organizations by locating Web pages for those organizations. Those Web pages generally contain links to their FTP servers or to specific files or directories on those servers. For example, while you may not be able to locate the IRS FTP server using Archie, you can easily locate it using any of the Web search services discussed in Project 3 (like Yahoo!, Magellan, or Infoseek) with search parameters such as Internal Revenue Service, Department of Revenue, or US Government. Once you have found the Web page, the FTP server won't be far off.

Most anonymous FTP servers are accessed through the Web. People surfing the Web often stumble upon an interesting Web page with a tantalizing link that says something like "Click here to download some cool stuff," and off you go into the wonderful world of FTP without even trying!

> **Tip** You can place a bookmark on any FTP servers (or even files or directories located on FTP servers) you encounter that may be useful in your job search. Yes, you can bookmark any kind of Internet document, not just Web pages!

Introducing Usenet Newsgroups

Usenet is a term that is actually older than the Internet itself. **Usenet** refers to an earlier system of interconnected mainframe computers that used standard telephone lines and early versions of desktop modems. Articles for discussion were transferred from one computer to another using this system. The term *Usenet* has persisted over the years, but newsgroups (the way in which the Usenet is organized) have come a long way both in the technology used to support their communications and in popularity.

Newsgroups are electronic discussion groups, where people with a common interest can carry on virtual conversations with each other. Each newsgroup generally limits the discussion to just one topic, but there are literally thousands of newsgroups on the Internet discussing everything from motorcycles to breast cancer to alien encounters to Buddhism to finding a job!

Netscape Communicator includes a component called Collabra which is specifically designed for newgroups.

Launching Netscape Collabra

Remember that all the components of Communicator are tightly integrated, so you can easily jump from one to another almost without noticing! Therefore, there are a number of ways to launch Netscape Collabra: if another component of Communicator is already running, you can choose Collabra Discussion Groups from the Communicator menu.

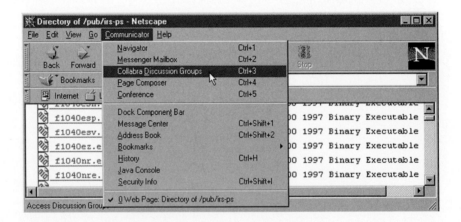

Or you can choose Discussions from the Communicator taskbar.

Alternatively, if Communicator is not already running, and depending upon the way in which Netscape Communicator is installed at your school, you may be able to launch Netscape Collabra directly from the Windows 95 start menu.

TASK 8: TO LAUNCH NETSCAPE COLLABRA

1 Use one of the three methods described above to launch Netscape Collabra.

Notice that Communicator opens the Message Center window. Remember the Message Center from Netscape Messenger? This is the very same window. As you may have already guessed, Collabra is very tightly integrated with Messenger, even sharing some windows.

As with using Netscape Messenger for e-mail, in order to use Collabra for newsgroups, it must be configured properly.

TASK 9: TO ACCESS NEWS PREFERENCES

1 Select Preferences from the Edit menu in the Message Center window.

The Preferences dialog box used for configuring Netscape Collabra for newsgroups (and Messenger for e-mail) appears.

TASK 10: TO CONFIGURE NEWS SERVERS PREFERENCES

1 Select the Groups Server tab on the Preferences dialog box.

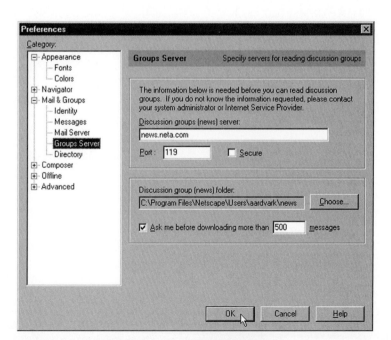

To use Messenger for e-mail, you had to specify your e-mail servers. The same is true for newsgroups—you must tell Collabra where to find your news (NNTP) server and where you want Collabra to store your news files.

2 If it is not already properly entered, get your instructor's help to enter the address of your news server in the News (NNTP) Server field.

The Discussion group (news) folder field should contain the name of the folder (or subdirectory) where Collabra will keep your newsgroup subscription and information files. Collabra may display a default here. Your instructor will help you to determine if the default is appropriate, of if you should designate a folder in your computer account at school.

3 With your instructor's help enter the path and name of your news directory in the Discussion group (news) folder field.

4 Select the [OK] button.

Notice that your news server is listed in the Message Center window.

Accessing Newsgroups Using Collabra

Now that you have Collabra configured for newsgroups, you are ready to browse through all the available newsgroups on your news server and select one or two that interest you.

TASK 11: TO BROWSE NEWSGROUP CATEGORIES

1 To see the newsgroups on your news server, choose Subscribe to Discussion Groups from the File menu in the Message Center window.

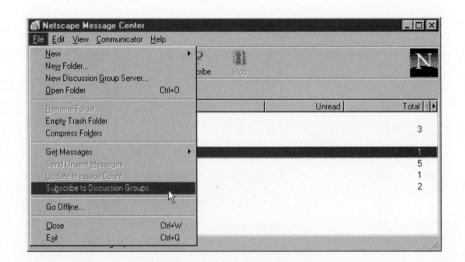

The Subscribe to Discussion Groups window appears. Collabra will now read the headers of all the newsgroups on your news server and display them in the Discussion Group Name list. This process may be immediate or may take a few minutes depending on the speed of the connection to your news server.

> **Don't Panic** if the newsgroups listed on your screen are different than those displayed in illustrations here. There is no standard list of newsgroups, and the list is always changing.

Notice that the newsgroups listed are grouped into folders. These folders or ***newsgroup categories*** contain a number of newsgroups that cover related topics. Table 7.2 lists just a few of the major newsgroup categories and the topics covered by each.

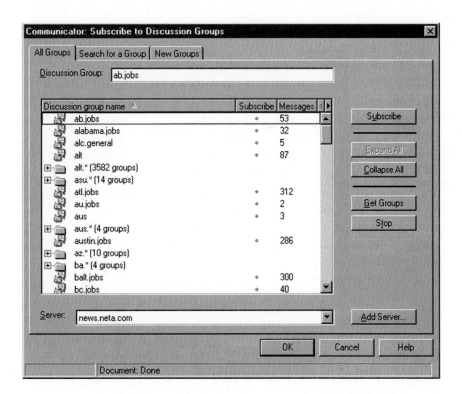

The number of newsgroups currently within each category is listed next to the category name in the Subscribe to Discussion Groups window. You can view a list of the newsgroups within a given category by selecting the plus sign (+) button to the left of the category folder icon.

2 Scroll through the list of displayed newsgroups and categories.

Table 7.2 A Few Major Newsgroup Categories

Document Type	Protocol and URL Format
alt.	Alternative—topics outside the mainstream and sometimes controversial
biz.	Business—topics related to the business world
comp.	Computers—topics concerned with computers
rec.	Recreational—topics related to recreational activities
sci.	Science—focuses on scientific issues
soc.	Social—focuses on debate over social issues

TASK 12: TO BROWSE NEWSGROUPS WITHIN A CATEGORY

1 Scroll down to the biz category of newsgroups.

2 Select the plus sign (+) button to the left of the biz. category folder icon.

The biz. category expands to a list of business-related newsgroups. Notice that there are subcategories of biz. These are folders within the biz category folder. Notice that the number of messages associated with each newsgroup appears under the postings header.

3 Scroll through the list of biz newsgroups to find a newsgroup or category related to jobs or employment.

4 If you find a jobs category within the biz. category, display the newsgroups within using its plus sign (+) button.

TASK 13: TO SUBSCRIBE TO A NEWSGROUP

1 Select the job-related newsgroup you found.

2 As shown in the following example, click the Subscribe field of the selected newsgroup.

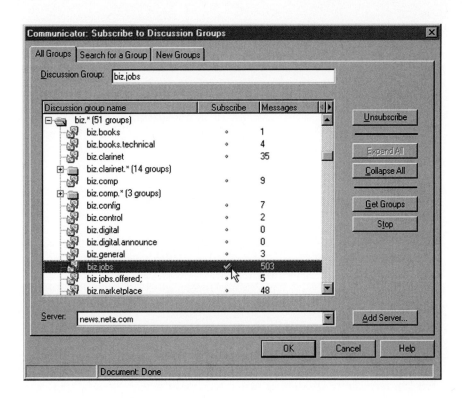

A check mark appears in the Subscribe field of the selected newsgroup. To cancel your subscription to the newsgroup, click the check mark, and it will disappear. For now though, leave this newsgroup subscribed so that you can view its messages.

3 Select the **OK** button.

Notice that the newsgroup to which you described is now listed beneath your news server in the Message Center window.

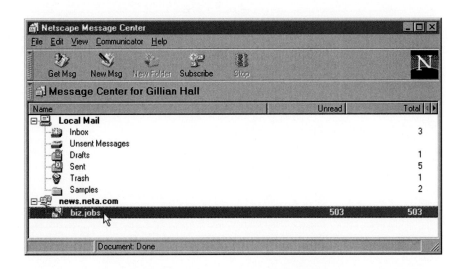

TASK 14: TO VIEW A NEWSGROUP MESSAGE

1 Double-click the subscribed newsgroup in the Message Center window.

Depending on the number of messages in the given newsgroup, Collabra may ask how many messages you want downloaded at a time.

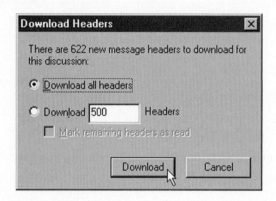

2 If the above dialog is displayed, make your downloading selections and, select the Download button.

Collabra will download the selected number of messages and display their headers in a message list window.

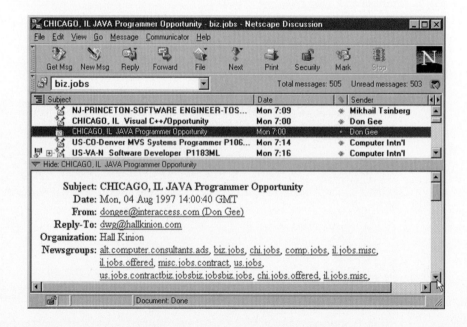

The Collabra message list window is virtually identical to the Messenger message list window. Notice that you can sort messages, display messages, get new messages, reply to, and forward messages in the same way as in the Messenger message list window.

3 Use the scroll bar to view the entire message displayed.

Remember that you may reply to this message using the same Reply button on the toolbar that you use to reply to e-mail. So if this job sounded good, you could just select the Reply button and send an e-mail message requesting an application packet from the company!

Once you have identified newsgroups like this one that have information in which you are interested, you may wish to subscribe. Subscribing to a newsgroup does not put you on any mailing lists, nor does it make you the member of any group. Subscribing to a newsgroup simply makes it easier for you to access messages in that group using Collabra.

The Conclusion

In this project you have learned about a few more resources available to you on the Internet: Gopher, FTP, and Usenet newsgroups. You also learned how to use Netscape Navigator and Collabra to access, search, and utilize these valuable resources.

This concludes Project 6. You can either exit Communicator or go on to work the Study Questions, Review Exercises, and Assignments.

Summary and Exercises

Summary

- Like Web pages, FTP and Gopher resources have special URL protocols—ftp: and gopher:, respectively.
- Gopher uses a hierarchical network of menus to guide you to text-based information resources on Gopher servers all over the world.
- Gopherspace is the complex network of interconnected Gopher menus.
- Many Gopher resources are being migrated to the Web due to its growing popularity.
- To access a Gopher server, you need to know its address (URL).
- Gopher menus are displayed in Navigator using menus of text links and icons indicating the types of links.
- File Transfer Protocol (FTP) is a means of passing from one computer to another.
- An FTP server is a computer that has made certain files available for downloading and certain directories available for uploading files.
- You can access an FTP server by using its URL or by selecting a link to an FTP server from a Web page.
- Netscape displays FTP servers using directory and file icons and text links to guide you through the hierarchy of directories.
- FTP servers provide many types of files, including graphics, programs, sounds, movies, text files, and more.
- Most files available on FTP servers are archived or compressed.
- Usenet newsgroups are electronic discussion groups.
- In order to access newsgroups using Collabra, you must configure a Groups server.
- You can view all newsgroups served by your news server using the Subscribe to Discussion Groups option in the Message Center File menu.
- Newsgroups are organized into categories and subcategories by discussion topics.
- You can subscribe to a newsgroup by selecting the Subscribe field.

Key Terms and Operations

Key Terms
archived file
category
compressed file
download
File Transfer Protocol (FTP)
Gopher
Gopher server
Gopherspace
newsgroup
self-extracting file
Usenet

Operations
navigate Gopher menus
navigate FTP directories
download a file
configure Discussions Server
open the Subscribe to Discussion Groups window
Browse newsgroup categories and newsgroups
subscribe to a newsgroup
browse newsgroup messages
view a message

Study Questions

Multiple Choice

1. The protocol portion of an URL tells you the _____ of the Internet document.
   a. size
   b. type
   c. age
   d. location

2. Gopher uses a hierarchical network of _____ to access resources.
   a. categories
   b. locations
   c. servers
   d. menus

3. When you are exploring the complex network of interconnected menus that make up the collection of Gopher servers, you are said to be tunneling through
   a. a rabbit warren.
   b. a worm hole.
   c. Gopherspace.
   d. cyberspace.

4. Gopher servers are currently _____ in number due to the growing popularity of the Web.
   a. increasing
   b. not changing
   c. decreasing
   d. exploding

5. Many resources that have previously been available on Gopher servers are being migrated to
   a. FTP servers.
   b. the Web.
   c. mainframe computers.
   d. CD-ROMs.

6. To subscribe to a newsgroup, click in the _____ field in the Subscribe to Discussion Groups dialog.
   a. select
   b. add
   c. subscribe
   d. get

7. FTP stands for
   a. File Transfer Paradigm.
   b. File Type Protocol.
   c. File Transfer Protocol.
   d. Fiberoptical Transfer Packet.

8. You _____ a file from an FTP server to a storage device on your local computer.
   a. translate
   b. upload
   c. download
   d. encrypt

9. A Usenet newsgroup is an electronic
   a. magazine.
   b. discussion group.
   c. news program.
   d. e-mail clearing house.

10. Newsgroups are organized into _____ based on the _____ of discussion for that newsgroup.
    a. categories, rating
    b. topics, subcategories
    c. topics, length
    d. categories, topic

Short Answer

1. _____ describes the complex interconnected network of Gopher menus on Gopher servers all over the world.

2. You can download a wide variety of software, images, and other computer resources from _____ servers.

3. Gopher menus are organized into _____.

4. You do not need a special password to log on and access a(n) _____ FTP server.

5. The directory in which most of the interesting downloadable files are kept on an FTP server is generally called _____.

6. In Netscape, you can begin downloading a file from an FTP server simply by _____ its icon.

7. To view a text file on an FTP server, without initiating the download process, you can _____ it.

8. You can get to Communicator's newsgroup component by selecting _____ from the Communicator menu.

9. You can keep better track of the discussion going on in a newsgroup by _____ to that newsgroup.

10. Before Netscape can access newsgroups, you must configure your _____ server.

For Discussion

1. Why are resources previously available on Gopher servers migrating to the Web?

2. What is the difference between Gopher and FTP? Give an example of information or resources you would consider looking for using each.

Review Exercises

1. Finding Job-Related Newsgroups

Use your Internet search services (try Yahoo!) or just explore the newsgroup categories.

1. Locate five more newsgroups that provide a forum for jobs offered.

2. Subscribe to the newsgroups you find.

3. Print one message from each of the news groups.

2. Reply to a Job Posting

Now that you have found a number of employment related newsgroups, browse through their messages and find five jobs that interest you.

1. Compose and send a reply to each of the job messages you find. For example, you may request more information or an application.

2. Print each of the messages you send using your Sent message list window.

Assignments

1. Use the Web for an FTP Search

Use your favorite search engine to search for PKZIP, a popular file compression application commonly available for download. Follow links provided by your search engine until you find a downloadable PKZIP file. Print the Web page on which you find a link for downloading the file.

2. Use Newsgroup Messages to Find Related Newsgroups

Look at the headers of a few messages posted in your favorite employment-related newsgroup. Notice that each message was sent to a number of newsgroups in addition to the one in which you found them. Subscribe to and browse through at least five employment-related newsgroups shown as additional recipients of these messages. Prepare a list of the employment newsgroups you located in this way. Print the list.

7

Creating Your Own Web Page with Composer

So how are all those Web pages you've visited throughout the projects in this book created? Most people think that creating Web pages is a complex and highly technical endeavor. In reality, the basics of Web page authoring are relatively simple; and Netscape Composer makes creating your own Web page easier than ever!

Objectives

After completing this project, you will be able to:

➤ **Launch Netscape Composer**

➤ **Access the Page Wizard and Templates**

➤ **Use Composer's text formatting tools**

➤ **Create links**

➤ **Save a Web page**

➤ **Preview a Web page with Navigator**

➤ **Publish a Web page**

The Challenge

You are rapidly approaching graduation and for the past few weeks have been busily learning how to use Netscape Communicator to access valuable job search resources on the Internet. In fact, you have probably spent more time recently learning about the Internet than you have polishing your resume. Never fear! Your big chance to show off your resume in its best light is here!

Actually, you have been hearing a lot of talk around campus about "my home page" this and "her home page" that. All this home page stuff sounds both intriguing and intimidating. But now that you have a solid foundation with the Internet using Netscape Communicator, you're beginning to wonder if creating your own Web page is really all that mysterious and difficult.

The Solution

You've used the Internet to find job opportunities and to communicate with prospective employers in a variety of ways. You have found the Web to be an excellent forum for conveying information. In fact, it has occurred to you that a Web page might be useful to you in your job search. What if you could include a link to your own personal Web page in e-mail messages to prospective employers? Complete with photos, an e-mail link, your resume, and links to universities you've attended and companies you've worked for, your own Web page might be very useful in your job search!

By the end of this project you will have the skills necessary to put together just such a Web page using Netscape Composer. But first you will be guided through the process of creating a Web page to organize the employment resources you have located during your travels on the Internet.

What Is Netscape Composer?

Earlier in this book, we mentioned that the Hypertext Markup Language (HTML) is a simple programming language used to create Web pages. *Netscape Composer* is an HTML authoring tool. It allows you to create richly formatted HTML documents viewable by Web browsers. The best part is that you don't need to learn HTML to use Composer. Instead of relying on your HTML coding skills, Composer works much like many familiar word processing applications. You simply type, and then apply styles to the text you have entered.

Launching Netscape Composer

Remember that all the components of Communicator are tightly integrated, so you can easily jump from one to another almost without noticing! Therefore, there are a number of ways to launch Netscape Composer. You can first launch Netscape Navigator 4.0 as covered in the Overview of this book, and then choose Page Composer from the Communicator menu.

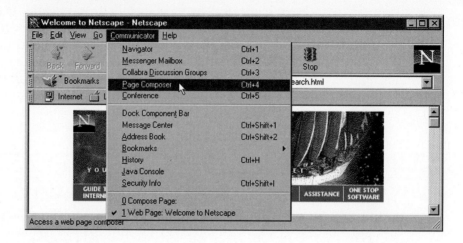

Or you can choose the Composer icon from the Communicator taskbar.

Alternatively, depending upon the way in which Netscape Communicator is installed at your school, you may be able to launch Netscape Composer directly from the Windows 95 start menu.

TASK 1: TO LAUNCH NETSCAPE COMPOSER

1. Click the Start button **Start** and point to Programs.

2. Point to the Netscape Communicator folder and then to Netscape Composer in the pull-down menus.

The Netscape Composer program is launched.

Just as when you launch Navigator, Messenger, Collabra, or Conference, the Netscape Communicator startup screen appears and remains on your screen while your computer establishes its connection to the network.

The startup screen disappears when a network connection has been confirmed. It is replaced by a Netscape Composer window and the Netscape Communicator taskbar.

Exploring the Composer Window

The Netscape Composer window is organized much like the main windows of other Communicator components. The Composer window includes a title bar, menu bar, toolbars, and scroll bars (when displaying pages that don't fit in the page composition area). These are all features you will find in nearly all Windows applications. The Composer window also includes other features important to composing Web pages including a text *formatting toolbar* and *page composition area*.

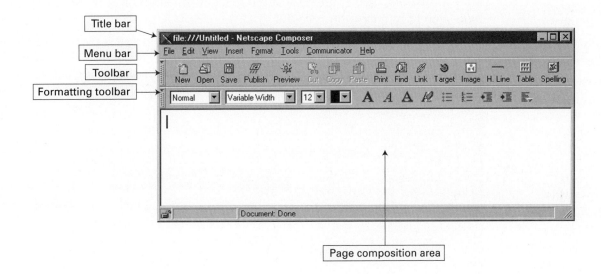

Getting Started

Netscape Composer allows you to start a Web page from scratch, modify an existing Web page, create a Web page using the *Netscape Page Wizard*, or use one of the *Netscape Web Page Templates*. In this project, we'll be creating a Web page from scratch.

TASK 2: TO ACCESS THE PAGE WIZARD

1 Choose New from the Composer File menu.

2 Choose Page From Wizard from the submenu that appears.

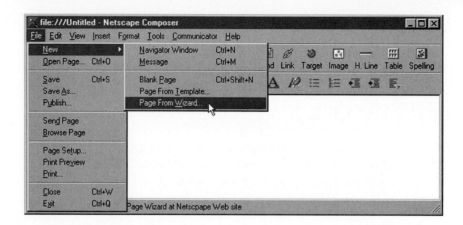

The Netscape Navigator is launched and the Netscape Page Wizard Web site is displayed. The Page Wizard guide's you through "fill-in-the-blank" style Web page creation process.

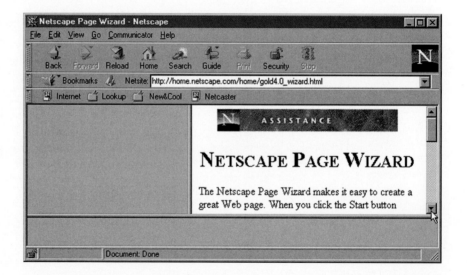

3   Close the browser window displaying the Netscape Page Wizard.

TASK 3: TO ACCESS PAGE TEMPLATES

1   Choose New from the Composer File menu.

2   Choose Page From Template from the submenu that appears.

The New Page From Template dialog appears.

3 Enter a location where you would like your new Web page to be saved.

4 Select the Netscape Templates button.

The Netscape Navigator is launched and the Netscape Web Page Templates site is displayed. The Web Page Templates site provides links to a number of Web pages that you can modify and use as starting points for your own Web page.

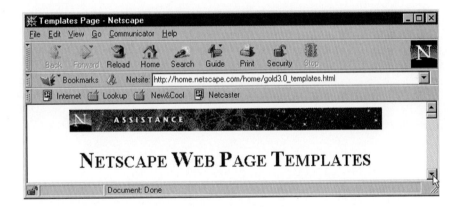

5 Scroll down to view the instructions for using the Web Page Templates.

6 Close the browser window displaying the Netscape Web Page Templates site.

Although the Wizard and Templates provide support for creating a Web page, they both encourage you to follow the page layouts provided by Netscape. A more flexible method for creating a Web page using Composer is to start from scratch. This is the method you will use to create your first Web page in this project.

TASK 4: TO START A NEW WEB PAGE FROM SCRATCH

1 Select the  button in the Composer toolbar.

The Create New Page dialog appears.

2 Select the [Blank Page] button.

A Composer window appears displaying a blank page composition area.

Using Composer's Text Formatting Tools

As already mentioned, using Composer to create a Web page is a lot like using a word processor. You simply type in the page composition area and use the text formatting toolbar to format your Web page.

Adding Text to a Web Page

Adding text to a Web page using Composer is as simple as typing.

TASK 5: TO ENTER TEXT ON YOUR WEB PAGE

1 Type **Job Search Resources** in the page composition area of the Composer window.

Creating Titles and Headings

You can transform any text you type into titles and headings by making selections from the paragraph and heading style menu in the formatting toolbar.

TASK 6: TO CREATE A TITLE

1 Choose Heading 1 from the paragraph and heading style menu in the formatting toolbar.

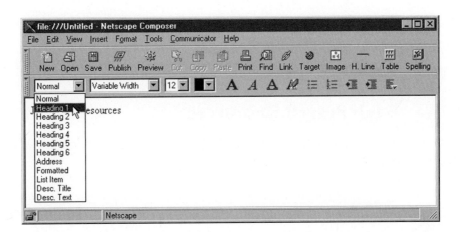

Notice that the text you entered is now displayed as a title in large, bold type.

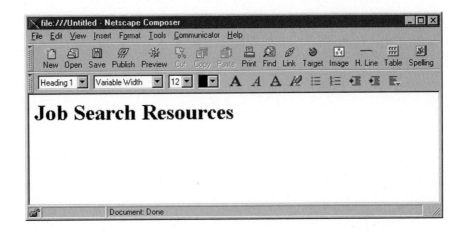

TASK 7: TO ADD A HEADING

1 Press ⒺⓃⓉⒺⓇ

2 Type **This page was developed to help job hunters locate the hottest sources of employment information on the Internet today!**

3 Choose Heading 4 from the paragraph and heading style menu.

Notice that the text you just typed is now displayed in bold type. This is the default style for Heading 4.

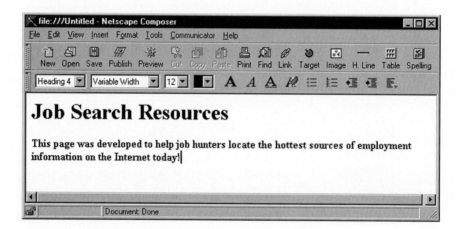

Changing Text Attributes

In the Overview you may recall that we discussed Navigator font preferences. Most browsers allow you to designate a default Variable Width and Fixed Width font. When you are designing a Web page, you can specify the font you want browsers to use when displaying your text. It is best to specify either Fixed or Variable Width fonts rather than specific type faces. This way, people will be able to view your page using their own browser font preferences.

TASK 8: TO SELECT A FONT

1 Select the title text on your Web page.

2 Choose Fixed Width from the font menu in the formatting toolbar.

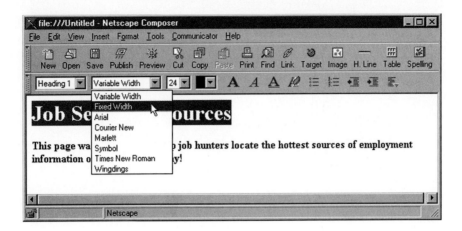

Notice that the title is now displayed in the Fixed Width font you specified in the Navigator font preferences.

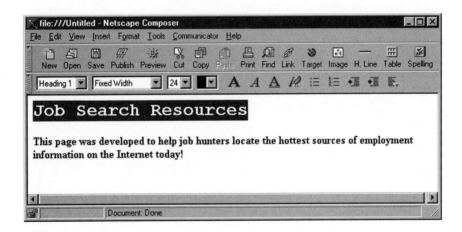

3 Choose Variable Width from the font menu to restore the title to a variable-width font.

TASK 9: TO SELECT FONT SIZE

1 Select the subheading text on your Web page.

2 Choose 14 from the font size menu in the formatting toolbar.

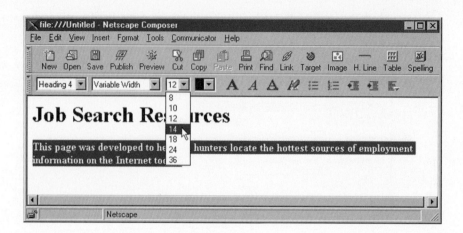

Notice that the text is now displayed in a 14 point font.

3 Change the font size of the selected text to 12 point.

TASK 10: TO SELECT TEXT COLOR

1 Select the title text on your Web page.

Composer allows you to choose from a menu of colors in which to display text. You can use color to highlight text or just to make your Web page more fun to read.

2 Choose Red from the font color menu in the formatting toolbar.

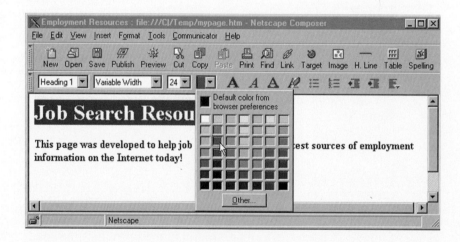

3 Deselect the title text by clicking elsewhere in the Composer window.

Notice that the title text is now displayed in red.

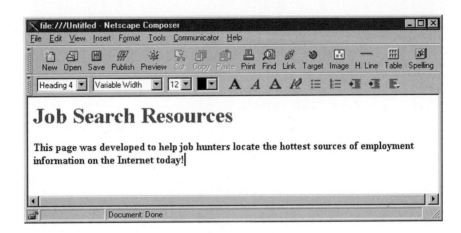

Composer also provides four text style buttons in the formatting toolbar—bold **A** , italic *A* , underscore A , and no style A . To apply any of these styles to text on your Web page, simply select the desired text and then select a style button.

TASK 11: TO SELECT TEXT STYLE

1 Select the subheading text on your Web page.

2 Choose the italic *A* button in the formatting toolbar.

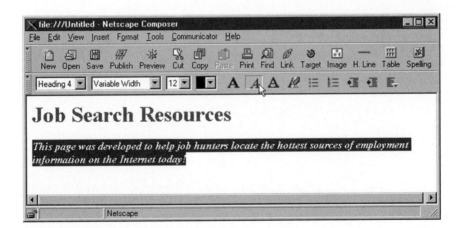

Notice that the subheading text is now displayed in italics.

3 Deselect the subheading text by clicking elsewhere in the Composer window.

TASK 12: TO REMOVE TEXT STYLES

1 Press (ENTER)

2 Type **Great Employment Web Sites**

Notice that the text you just typed is also displayed in italics. To remove the italics style from the text, you can use the Remove All Styles button.

3 Select the text you just typed.

4 Select the button.

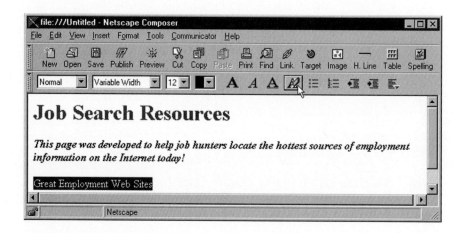

The selected text is displayed without any styles.

Before going on, use the paragraph and heading style menu to change Great Employment Web Sites to a Heading 3. Great Employment Web Sites will be used as the heading for a bulleted list of employment Web sites you have found so far in your job search.

Creating Bulleted and Numbered Lists

Lists are a great way to present information on a Web page in an organized way. On your Employment Resources Web page, you will use lists to present and organize some of the Internet job search resources you have found.

TASK 13: TO CREATE A BULLETED LIST

1 Deselect any selected text, and make sure your insertion point is at the end of the subheading, Great Employment Web Sites.

2   Press Ⓔⁿᵀᴱᴿ

3   Select the bulleted list button ⊞

An indented bullet appears on your page.

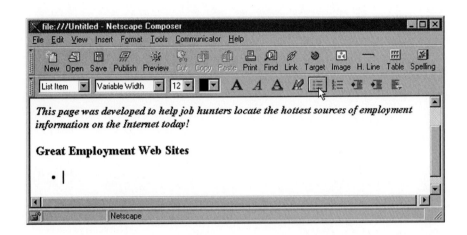

4   Type **JobWeb**

5   Press Ⓔⁿᵀᴱᴿ

6   Type the names of at least two other employment Web sites you have bookmarked. Press Ⓔⁿᵀᴱᴿ after each name.

7   After entering all of your Web site names as items in your bulleted list, select the ⊞ button to end the list.

TASK 14: TO CREATE A NUMBERED LIST

1   Type **Employment Newsgroups**, and make this text a Heading 3 using the paragraph and heading style menu in the formatting toolbar.

2   Press Ⓔⁿᵀᴱᴿ

3   Select the numbered list button ⊞

An indented # sign appears on your page. The # signs in numbered lists are replaced by numbers (i.e., 1, 2, 3, . . .) when the page is viewed with a Web browser.

4   Type **biz.jobs.offered**

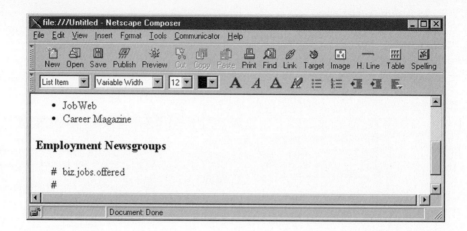

5 Press (ENTER)

6 Type the names of at least one other employment-related newsgroup you have found. Press (ENTER) after each name.

7 After entering all of your newsgroup names as items in your numbered list, select the 🔲 button to end the list.

Changing Text Alignment

You can change text alignment using the text alignment tools in the formatting toolbar. Composer offers centered, right justified, and left justified text alignment options.

TASK 15: TO CHANGE TEXT ALIGNMENT

1 Select the title text on your Web page.

2 Select the alignment button 🔲

3 Choose centered text from the pull-down menu.

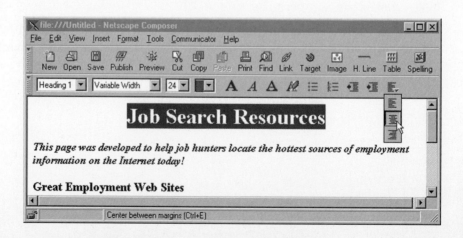

Your Web page title is centered in the page composition area.

4 Deselect the title bar.

Creating Links on Your Web Page

You have created two lists on your Web page. One list shows some of the employment Web sites you have found and the other lists some employment-related newsgroups. To make your Web page more useful, it would be nice if each item in these lists were linked to the page or newsgroup named.

TASK 16: TO CREATE TEXT LINKS

1 Select the first item in the bulleted list.

2 Select the link button

The Character Properties dialog appears displaying Link properties. All you need to do is enter the URL of the JobWeb home page in the field provided as shown below.

3 Type **http://www.jobweb.com** in the field provided.

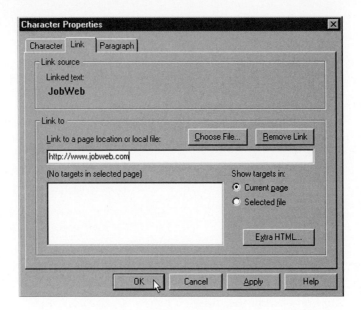

4 Select the OK button.

JobWeb is now displayed as a text link.

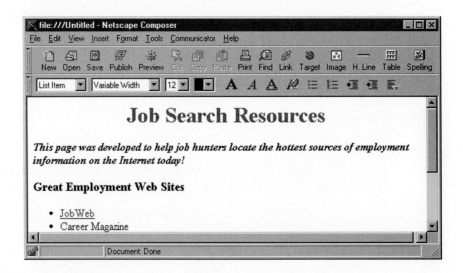

Saving Your Web Page

When you have finished working on your Web page, it is important to save your work.

TASK 17: TO SAVE YOUR WEB PAGE

1 Choose Save As from the Composer File menu.

The Windows 95 Save As dialog appears.

2 Select a location, and enter a file name (e.g., mypage) in the field provided.

3 Select the [Save] button.

The Page Title dialog will appear the first time you save your page.

4 Type **Employment Resources** in the field provided.

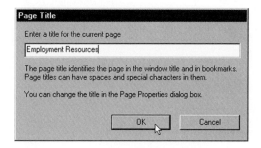

5 Select the [OK] button.

Previewing Your Web Page

You can open and view your Web page in Navigator to make sure it looks the way you intended. There are a number of ways to do this. You can open the page directly from Navigator by choosing Open Page from the File menu. Another method is to select the Preview button on the Composer toolbar.

TASK 18: TO PREVIEW YOUR WEB PAGE

1 Select the Preview button [Preview] on the Composer toolbar.

Navigator is launched and your Web page is displayed in the browser window.

2 When you are finished previewing your Web page, close the browser window.

Publishing Your Web Page

You may have heard the term *publishing* used in conjunction with the Web. **Publishing** on the Web simply means making some information resource you have created available on the Web. The Web page you have created is not published and cannot be accessed by others until you find it a permanent home.

TASK 19: TO PUBLISH YOUR WEB PAGE

 Select the publish button on the Composer toolbar.

The Publish dialog appears. You must now specify the location to which your Web page and its associated files will be copied. This will probably be the address of your school computer account. You will also need to enter your user name and password. If you need help, your instructor will assist you in completing the necessary fields.

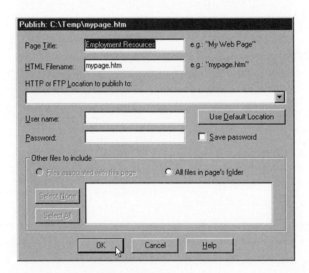

2 Select the OK button, and Composer will publish your Web page.

The Conclusion

In this project you have learned to use some of Composer's tools to create and publish your own Web page. This will be a valuable tool in your job search both to help keep track of employment resources on the Internet and to present your qualifications to prospective employers.

This concludes Project 7. You can either exit Communicator or go on to work the Study Questions, Review Exercises, and Assignments.

Summary and Exercises

Summary

- Netscape Composer is an HTML authoring tool.
- You can launch Composer from the Communicator menu, the taskbar, or the Start menu.
- The Web page is created in the Composer page composition area.
- With Composer, you don't need to know any HTML.
- Netscape provides a Page Wizard and Web Page Templates which make creating a Web page with Composer even easier.
- Starting a new Web page from scratch gives you more flexibility than using the Wizard or a Template.
- The paragraph and heading style menu in the formatting toolbar allows you to apply heading styles to selected text.
- Rather than specifying specific fonts, it is better to use generic font descriptions such as fixed width and variable width.
- You can change the size of selected text using the font size menu in the formatting toolbar.
- A color menu in the formatting toolbar allows you to change the color of selected text.
- Composer provides a number of text style buttons on the formatting toolbar.
- To create a bulleted or numbered list, simply select the desired button on the formatting toolbar.
- To end a list, select the list button again.
- Composer allows you to center, left justify, or right justify text using the align text menu.
- To create a text link, select the text you wish to turn into a link, and then select the link button in the Composer toolbar.
- You can preview a saved Web page in a Preview window by selecting the browse button in the Composer toolbar.
- To publish your Web page, you must provide the address, user name, and password for the location to which you want the page published.

Key Terms and Operations

Key Terms
formatting toolbar
Netscape Composer
Netscape Page Wizard
Netscape Web Page Template
page composition area
publish

Operations
launch Composer
access the Page Wizard
access Page Templates
create new blank page
use text formatting toolbar
create links
save page
preview page
publish page

Study Questions _____

Multiple Choice

1. All good Web pages should contain
   a. links to related documents.
   b. many large graphic files.
   c. None of the above.
   d. Both a and b.

2. Netscape Composer is a(n) _____ authoring tool.
   a. HTTP
   b. FTP
   c. HTML
   d. Gopher

3. You can create a Web page using Composer in much the same way you would create a document using a _____ application.
   a. spreadsheet
   b. word processing
   c. page layout
   d. photo rendering

4. The Netscape Page _____ provides a structured, "fill-in-the-blank" approach to Web page creation.
   a. Template
   b. Wizard
   c. Writer
   d. Sorcerer

5. Netscape _____ provide(s) a starting point for creating your own Web pages by allowing you to edit prepared pages.
   a. Web Page Templates
   b. Page Wizard
   c. Composer page compostion area
   d. All of the above.

6. To create a new page using Composer, select _____ from the _____ menu.
   a. New Page; Author
   b. New; File
   c. New; Edit
   d. New Page; Communicator

7. Instead of selecting specific fonts for your Web page, it is better to designate _____ or _____ font.
   a. Fixed Width; Variable Width
   b. Times; Courier
   c. bold; underscore
   d. bold; italic

8. You can use the font _____ menu in the text formatting toolbar to change the color of selected text.
   a. style
   b. size
   c. color
   d. face

9. Composer offers _____, _____, and _____ text style buttons.
   a. bold; plain; italic
   b. bold; strikeout; italic
   c. bold; italic; underscore
   d. bold; plain; none

10. Use the desired _____ button to begin or end a _____.
   a. bullet; list
   b. indent bulleted list
   c. alignment; list
   d. list; list

Short Answer

1. Netscape _____ are Web pages you can modify to suit your own needs.

2. You can use the Netscape _____ if you want to be guided through the Web page authoring process.

3. You can change the _____ of text using the _____ menu to highlight or add interest to your Web page.

4. The _____ button removes all styles from selected text.

5. Composer provides buttons for creating _____ and _____ lists.

6. Create a text link on your Web page by _____ the desired text and selecting the _____ button.

7. Before publishing your Web page, you may wish to _____ it using your Web _____.

8. When saving a Web page for the first time, Composer will ask you for a page _____ to display in the browser title bar.

9. To publish a Web page using Composer, you need the _____, _____, and _____ for the location to which you wish to publish the page.

10. A Web page is considered to be _____ when anyone can access it over the Internet.

For Discussion

1. You know that HTML is a programming language in which all Web pages are written. But in this project you haven't seen a single line of HTML. Does Composer write HTML for you? Is there any way to view the HTML code generated for your Web page?

2. Netscape provides a number of Web page templates that may help you to create your own Web page. Wouldn't it be nice to be able to use any page you find on the Web as a template for your own page? Can you do this with Composer?

Review Exercises

1. Adding More Links to Your Web Page

You already added one link to your Employment Resources Web page. Now you can finish the job!

1. Create links for each item in the two lists on your Web page.

2. Save your Web page.

3. Print your Web page using the Print button in the Composer toolbar.

2. Hook Up to Some Search Services

Now let's add some helpful search features to your Web page.

1. Create another subheading to your Web page called "Search Services."

2. Create a bulleted list beneath the new subheading and enter the names of at least three search services as items in the list.

3. Make each of the items in the list into text links to the search services named.

4. Save your Web page.

5. Print your Web page using the Print button in the Composer toolbar.

Assignments

1. Your Bio Online!

Build a new Web page from scratch. This page must contain a heading of your choosing (e.g., Professional Resume, etc.), and introduction including a brief biography, your resume (formatted nicely using Composer's text formatting tools), and at least one link (e.g., a link to your school's Web page, to an employer's Web page, or to your e-mail address). Print your Web page in Composer.

2. Check Out the HTML Source Code

View the HTML source code that Composer generated for the Web page created in Assignment 1. Use online help if you need assistance. Print your Web page's source code.

Operations Reference

The following command reference covers only menu options, buttons, and actions discussed in this *SELECT Lab Series* module.

Collabra Menus

See Messenger Menus.

Communicator Menus

Communicator

Button	Menu Option	Keyboard	Description
	Navigator	CTRL + 1	Goes to Netscape Navigator.
	Messenger Mailbox	CTRL + 2	Goes to Netscape Messenger.
	Collabra Discussion Groups	CTRL + 3	Goes to Netscape Collabra.
	Page Composer	CTRL + 4	Goes to Netscape Composer.
	Conference	CTRL + 5	Goes to Netscape Conference.
☒	Dock Component Bar		Docks the Communicator taskbar in the lower right corner of all Communicator windows.
	Message Center	CTRL + SHIFT + 1	Displays the Message Center window.
	Address Book	CTRL + SHIFT + 2	Displays the Address Book window.
Bookmarks	Bookmarks		Adds, files, edits, views, and uses bookmarks.
	History	CTRL + H	Displays the History window.
	various open windows		Allows you to select from the list displayed to go to a currently open window.

Help

Button	Menu Option	Keyboard	Description
	Help Contents	F1	Displays online Help contents.

Composer Menus

File

Button	Menu Option	Keyboard	Description
New	New		Creates a new blank Web page, or creates a new Web page using a template or the Page Wizard.
Open	Open Page...	(CTRL) + O	Opens an existing page.
Save	Save	(CTRL) + S	Saves the currently open page.
	Save As...		Saves a page using a new name.
Publish	Publish...		Publishes the currently displayed page.

Format

Button	Menu Option	Keyboard	Description
Variable Width	Font		Selects the desired font.
14	Size		Selects a font size.
A A A	Style		Selects a font style.
■	Color		Selects a font color.
Save	Remove All Styles	(CTRL) + K	Removes all font styles.
Heading 3	Heading		Selects a heading size.
Heading 3	Paragraph		Selects a paragraph style.
	List		Creates a numbered or bulleted list.
	Align		Selects a text alignment.

Insert

Button	Menu Option	Keyboard	Description
Link	Link	(CTRL) + (SHIFT) +L	Inserts a new link in a Web page.

Conference Menus

Conference Whiteboard Window

File

Button	Menu Option	Keyboard	Description
Print	Print		Prints the Whiteboard.
X	Close	(ALT) + (F4)	Closes the Whiteboard window.

Edit

Button	Menu Option	Keyboard	Description
	Clear Whiteboard		Clears the contents of the Whiteboard.

Conference File Exchange Window

File

Button	Menu Option	Keyboard	Description
	Add to send list	CTRL + A	Selects file to send.
	Close	ALT + F4	Closes the File Exchange window.

Conference Text Chat Window

File

Button	Menu Option	Keyboard	Description
	Print		Prints the chat log file.
	Close	ALT + F4	Closes the Chat Tool window.

Messenger Menus

Message Center Window

File

Button	Menu Option	Keyboard	Description
	New Folder...		Creates a new e-mail folder.
	Subscribe to Discussion Groups...		Opens the Subscribe to Discussion Groups dialog from which newsgroups can be selected for subscription.

Message List Window

File

Button	Menu Option	Keyboard	Description
	New Message	CTRL + M	Opens a message composition window.
	Empty Trash Folder		Empties the Trash folder.

Button	Menu Option	Keyboard	Description
	Get Messages		Retrieves new messages from the e-mail server.
	Close	CTRL + W	Closes the message composition window.
	Exit	CTRL + Q	Exits Netscape Communicator.

Edit

Button	Menu Option	Keyboard	Description
	Delete Message	DELETE	Moves the selected message to the Trash folder.

View

Button	Menu Option	Keyboard	Description
	Hide Message		Hides the message display area.
	Sort		Sorts messages by one of the available headers.
	Stop Loading	ESC	Stops downloading the currently loading e-mail messages.

Message

Button	Menu Option	Keyboard	Description
	Reply	CTRL + R	Opens a message composition window for a reply to the selected message.
	Forward	CTRL + L	Opens a message composition window with the selected message as an attachment.

Message Composition Window

File

Button	Menu Option	Keyboard	Description
	Send Now	CTRL + ENTER	Sends the displayed message.
	Quote Original Text		Includes text of original message with a reply.
	Select Addresses...		Accesses the Address Book from which recipient addresses may be selected.
	Attach		Attaches a computer file to the e-mail message for transmission with the message to its recipient.

Button	Menu Option	Keyboard	Description
[×]	Close	CTRL + W	Closes the message composition window.
	Exit	CTRL + Q	Exits Netscape Communicator.

Edit

Button	Menu Option	Keyboard	Description
	Undo	CTRL + Z	Undoes last action.
	Cut	CTRL + X	Cuts selected text to the clipboard.
	Copy	CTRL + C	Copies selected text to the clipboard.
	Paste	CTRL + V	Pastes clipboard text to the selected location.

Tools

Button	Menu Option	Keyboard	Description
[Spelling]	Check Spelling		Checks spelling in e-mail message body.

Navigator Menus

Navigator Window

File

Button	Menu Option	Keyboard	Description
	Open Page...	CTRL + O	Lets you type a URL or to select a file to display in the page display area.
	Page Setup...		Displays the Page Setup dialog in which you can specify printing characteristics of subsequent printing operations.
	Print Preview		Displays a screen image of how the printed page will look.
[Print]	Print...		Displays the print dialog allowing you to print the currently displayed page or frame.
[×]	Close	CTRL + W	Closes the active window.
	Exit	CTRL + Q	Exits Netscape Communicator.

Edit

Button	Menu Option	Keyboard	Description
	Find in Page (Frame)...	CTRL + F	Displays the Find dialog from which you can specify text to find in the currently displayed page or frame.
	Find Again	CTRL + G	Finds the next instance of the text entered in the Find dialog box.
Search	Search Internet		Displays the Internet Search page.
	Preferences...		Displays the Preferences window.

View

Button	Menu Option	Keyboard	Description
	Hide Navigation Toolbar		Hides the Navigation Toolbar.
	Hide Location Toolbar		Hides the Location Toolbar.
	Hide Personal Toolbar		Hides the Personal Toolbar.
Reload	Reload	CTRL + R	Reloads the current page.
Stop	Stop Page Loading	ESC	Stops downloading the current page.

Go

Button	Menu Option	Keyboard	Description
Back	Back	ALT + ←	Goes to the last page displayed.
Forward	Forward	ALT + →	Goes to the next page in the current session history.
Home	Home		Goes to the designated home page.
	locations visited in current session		Selects from the list displayed to go to a location already visited.

Bookmarks Window

File

Button	Menu Option	Keyboard	Description
	New Bookmark...		Creates a bookmark for the current page.
	New Folder...		Creates a new bookmarks folder.
	Save As...	CTRL + S	Saves your bookmarks to a file.
	Close	CTRL + W	Closes the Bookmarks window.

Edit

Button	Menu Option	Keyboard	Description
	Undo	(CTRL) + Z	Undoes the last action.
	Redo	(CTRL) + E	Redoes the last undone action.
	Delete	(DELETE)	Deletes the selected item.

Glossary

Address Book Communicator's facility for storing and retrieving frequently used e-mail addresses.

anonymous An FTP server that allows any Internet user to download files.

archived file A computer file or collection of files that have been compressed and stored for future use.

ARPAnet A computer network designed by the U.S. Defense Department in 1969 to ensure that its computers could communicate with one other.

attachment A computer file sent to its recipient by attaching it to an e-mail message.

backbone One of the many massive communication lines that connects major portions of the Internet.

body (e-mail) The part of an e-mail message that contains the message itself.

bookmark A Netscape Navigator tool for permanently marking favorite places on the Internet.

bottom-up search strategy With regard to Internet search services, a method of searching for a specific key word or phrase (i.e., beginning a search at the lowest level).

category Usenet newsgroups are organized into major categories (e.g., biz., alt., rec., comp.), some of which are further organized into subcategories.

CD-ROM Compact disk read-only memory, a popular medium for storing and accessing large archives of information using a computer.

chat tool A Netscape Conference tool used to conduct online text-based conversations and meetings.

collaborative browsing tool A Netscape Conference tool used to control another person's Navigator Web browser remotely in order to display material for discussion.

column Some Communicator windows are organized into labeled columns (e.g., date, subject, sender).

component bar Short cuts for accessing Communicator's most commonly used tools.

compressed file A computer file that has been subjected to a compression routine rendering it smaller and more efficient to archive and transmit. Compressed files must be decompressed before they can be used.

containers Netscape Messenger allows you to organize and store e-mail messages within containers or folders.

digital line Communication lines between computers using digital signals. Digital communication is much easier and more effective for computers because all data stored and used internally is in digital format.

directory A topic-driven search service provided on the Internet.

domain name The unique name given to each computer on the Internet. These names are translated into unique domain addresses by domain servers.

download To copy a file from a computer on the Internet to a local storage device (e.g., diskette, hard drive) on your computer, usually via FTP.

dynamic lookup service An Internet server that keeps track of Internet users currently online and their IP addresses.

e-mail Short for electronic mail, the most popular use of the Internet. It allows you to send messages and files to other Internet users.

file exchange tool A Netscape Conference tool used to exchange computer files over the Internet.

file name The portion of an Internet address that designates a specific file (in a specified directory on a specified computer).

File Transfer Protocol (FTP) One of the original sets of rules on the Internet that provides efficient file transfers between computers.

fixed-width fonts Fonts whose characters each occupy the same amount of horizontal space (e.g., Courier).

folder (bookmark) A method used by Netscape Navigator to organize bookmarks into groups.

formatting (e-mail) Specifying colors, fonts, and even including graphics for use in e-mail messages.

formatting toolbar The Netscape Composer and Messenger toolbar providing a number of text formatting tools.

fully duplex communication Electronic communication in which you can both send and receive at the same time.

gateway A device that connects two networks whose communication protocols are different.

Gopher An older method of indexing, publishing, and navigating Internet files.

Gopher server Computer systems running Gopher software allowing file access through hierarchical text-based menus arranged by subject.

Gopherspace   The collection of Gopher servers available on the Internet.

header (e-mail)   The portion of the e-mail message containing the components such as date, time, sender name and address, and subject.

history   Netscape Navigator's method of keeping track of where you've been on the Internet during the current session.

home page   A starting point (URL) for Web browsers to contact a person's, company's, or organization's information on the Web.

hypermedia links   Web page links to text, graphic, video, and sound files.

hypertext links   A means of connecting multiple files together via Web page links to create a single virtual document.

Hypertext Markup Language (HTML)   The formatting system that turns ordinary text files into Web pages.

Internet   The vast system of interconnected computers that Netscape navigates.

Internet Protocol (IP)   A set of rules that allows long data streams to be divided into small chunks that can be serialized, addressed, and sent to locations by different routes where they are reassembled into the original data stream.

link   An element on the Web that connects one part of a document to another part of that same document, or to another document or file. Links can connect files located on the same computer or on different computers connected to the Internet.

location field   In Netscape Navigator, the location field displays the Internet address of the currently displayed document. It is also used to enter the address of a document you wish to display.

menu bar   The part of a Windows 95 application window displaying pull-down menus.

Message Center   The Netscape Messenger and Collabra facility in which e-mail containers, news servers, and subscribed newsgroups are displayed.

message display area   The portion of the Netscape Messenger window that displays the selected e-mail message.

message header area   The portion of the Netscape Messenger window that displays the headers of all e-mail messages contained in the selected folder.

modem   A modulating demodulating device that allows computers to send and receive digital data over analog phone lines.

MS-DOS   Microsoft Disk Operating System, a popular disk operating system used on many personal computers.

Netscape Collabra   The Netscape Communicator component dedicated to Internet discussion groups.

Netscape Communicator   A collection of five tightly integrated Internet tools designed to access and use Internet resources and technology for communication and collaboration.

Netscape Composer   The Netscape Communicator component dedicated to creating and publishing Web content.

Netscape Conference   The Netscape Communicator component dedicated to Internet collaboration including a shared whiteboard, chat tool, file exchange tool, Internet telephone, and collaborative Web browsing tool.

Netscape Messenger   The Netscape Communicator component dedicated to sending, receiving, and managing electronic mail (e-mail).

Netscape Navigator 4.0   The Web browsing component of Netscape Communicator. Navigator is used for accessing and exploring the Internet. *See also Web browser.*

Netscape Page Wizard   An online Netscape resource allowing you to create Web pages with Netscape Composer using a step-by-step guided approach.

Netscape Web Page Template   An online Netscape resource allowing you to create Web pages with Netscape Composer by selecting from a collection prepared templates and customizing these templates to suit your needs.

newsgroup   One of thousands of discussion groups on the Usenet where people with a common interest share information.

online Help   A Netscape Communicator facility that provides Communicator users with a complete tutorial and reference via the Internet.

page composition area   The area of the Netscape Composer window in which the content of a Web page is developed.

page display area   The portion of the Netscape Navigator window in which an Internet document is displayed.

password   A secret set of characters you use to gain access to your computer account.

picture link   A link on a Web page whose anchor is a graphic.

POP server   POP stands for Post Office Protocol. This is the e-mail system that handles your incoming mail.

progress bar   The bar at the bottom of Communicator windows that displays the application's current communications status.

protocol   A set of rules by which computers communicate with each other.

publish   In regard to Web pages, publishing refers to making a Web page available to others on the Internet.

quoting   Replying to an e-mail message with the text of the original message included in the reply.

real time   In the present, not delayed. Performing tasks over the Internet, for example.

scroll bar   A special type of control that allows the user to easily navigate through a long list of information. There are vertical and horizontal scroll bars.

search engine   A keyword Internet search tool.

search parameter   Keywords or other user input used by search engines to search for documents on the Internet.

search strategy   The way in which a search service functions (e.g., keyword search, topic search).

self-extracting file   A compressed file that can decompress itself without requiring a separate utility application to do so.

signature   The portion of an e-mail message containing information about the sender. A signature sometimes includes an e-mail link or a trademark phrase.

SMTP server   Simple Mail Transport Protocol system that handles your outgoing e-mail.

stand-alone   With regard to computer software applications, stand-alone indicates an application that can be installed and used independent of other applications.

status indicator   The Netscape icon displayed in the upper right corner of Communicator windows. The animation of this icon indicates that Communicator is currently downloading data. The status indicator can be clicked to go to the Netscape home page.

text link   A link on a Web page whose anchor is text.

title bar   The part of an MS Windows application window containing the name of the window or of the document displayed in the window.

toolbar   The row of buttons in the Netscape window which provide short cuts for accessing frequently used menu options.

top-down search strategy   The search strategy employed by Internet directories. Top-down means that the search begins with a broad category and progresses to greater levels of specificity.

topic   Internet directories perform searches by topic. The user selects a topic from the top level of the directory, then selects a subtopic from each successive list of subtopics until a list of matching Internet documents is reached.

Trash folder   Temporary storage for deleted e-mail messages.

Uniform Resource Locator (URL)   The unique address assigned to every document accessible on the Web.

Usenet   A worldwide network exchanging information grouped under subject categories called newsgroups.

user name   The name assigned to an account on a computer on a local network or on the Internet. Usually, both the user name and password are necessary to access a computer account.

variable-width fonts   Fonts whose characters occupy a varied amount of horizontal space (e.g., Times).

voice conferencing tool   The Netscape Conference tool facilitating real-time Internet voice communication, like an Internet telephone.

voice mail   A broad term referring to leaving a voice message for someone either electronically or on a telephone answering system.

Web authoring   Creating content for the World Wide Web, or creating Web pages.

Web browser   An application used to access the World Wide Web. Netscape Navigator is a graphical Web browser.

Web page   A document written in HTML which is readable by a Web browser. *See also Hypertext Markup Language (HTML).*

whiteboard tool   The Netscape Conference tool used for collaboration on creating and marking up graphic images.

World Wide Web   An arrangement of Internet-accessible resources interconnected through hypertext and hypermedia and addressed by URLs. Also referred to as the Web.

Index